Co

G

First published in 2008 by
Collins, an imprint of
HarperCollins Publishers
77–85 Fulham Palace Road
London, W6 8JB

www.collins.co.uk

Collins Gem is a registered trademark of HarperCollins Publishers Limited

Reprint 10 9 8 7 6 5 4 3 2 1 0

© HarperCollins*Publishers* 2008

Based on material from *Collins need to know? Golf*

A catalogue record for this book is available from the British Library

Created by: SP Creative Design
Editor: Heather Thomas
Designer: Rolando Ugolini

Photographer: Rolando Ugolini

ISBN: 978 0 00 726237 3

Printed and bound by Amadeus S.r.l., Italy

Mixed Sources
Product group from well-managed
forests and other controlled sources
www.fsc.org Cert no. SW-COC-1806
© 1996 Forest Stewardship Council

FSC is a non-profit international organisation established to promote the
responsible management of the world's forests. Products carrying the FSC
label are independently certified to assure consumers that they come
from forests that are managed to meet the social, economic and
ecological needs of present and future generations.

Find out more about HarperCollins and the environment at
www.harpercollins.co.uk/green

CONTENTS

CHOOSING GOLF CLUBS

Golfers' physical builds differ, so we need different clubs.
When choosing clubs, consider your height, arm, leg and
body length, hand size, strength and natural rhythm;
they all influence how you swing and the clubs to use.

LIE OF THE CLUB

This is the angle between
the sole of the club head
and the shaft. If it is not
correct, then the heel or
toe of an iron will dig into

These 5 iron clubs come in flat,
standard or upright lie options.
Note how the soles of all three
clubs sit flat on the ground.

QUICK TIP: Which should I use?

If you are tall and your fingertips are more than 72cm (29in)
from the ground when standing erect, your clubs should be
more upright than standard; if they're less than 70cm (27in),
you need flatter lie clubs. If you fall into either category,
adopt the correct posture in your set up (see page 28)
to establish the degree of alteration from standard.

the ground, causing the club head to twist at impact. Your height and arm length will determine whether you need standard lie clubs.

LOFT AND SHAFT LENGTHS

Golf clubs fall into two groups: woods and irons. Woods now have shafts constructed of stainless steel, graphite and titanium. Although steel shafts are accurate and less expensive, graphite and titanium add weight to the club head, creating higher, more powerful shots that travel further. The loft and shaft length vary with each club. As loft increases by increments of four degrees, the shaft length decreases by 1.25cm ($^1/_2$in) per club.

QUICK TIP: Which loft is right for you?

Children up to 12 years	15 degrees of loft
Children 12–14 years	13 degrees of loft
Boys 14–16 years	11 degrees of loft
Girls 14–16 years	12 degrees of loft
Men below 8 handicap*	8–10 degrees of loft
Women below 8 handicap*	10–11 degrees of loft
Men 8–20 handicap*	10–12 degrees of loft
Women 8–20 handicap*	11–12 degrees of loft
Men above 20 handicap	13–15 degrees of loft
Women above 20 handicap	13–15 degrees of loft

*Add one degree if aged over 50 and two degrees if over 60.

CLUB HEAD DESIGN

You are unlikely to strike the ball right in the centre of the club face all the time, so use a club whose weight is distributed around the perimeter of the head, making the sweet spot (the part of the club face that, when a ball is hit correctly, produces the best shot) bigger and allowing you to get away with an off-centre hit

Irons loft table

(in degrees)

Club	Men	Ladies
No 2	19°	–
No 3	23°	24°
No 4	27°	28°
No 5	31°	32°
No 6	35°	36°
No 7	39°	40°
No 8	43°	44°
No 9	47°	48°

Pro/tournament irons are usually one degree less than mens' irons.

Blades versus iron club heads

Blades are more suitable for low-handicappers and pros. Beginners should use a cast iron club head of hard steel. More advanced players may benefit from forged clubs made of mild steel for a more controlled ball flight.

Three distinctly different designs of iron heads. From the top: a forged blade; a forged heel and toe weighted club; and a cast heel and toe weighted club (harder steel).

SHAFT FLEX

Make sure you get this right as choosing the wrong shaft flex can harm your swing and lead to mishits. The flexes available are: ladies'; flexible men's; regular; stiff; and extra stiff. The shaft is the powerhouse of the club, transferring the power of your swing to the club head. Your strength, hand action and swing speed will determine which flex you need. A slow swing is better suited to more flexible shafts, but stiffer shafts are better if you are strong with a fast swing.

Older golfers may not have the physical strength and flexibility of younger players. If you are a senior with a slow swing, you should play with clubs with more flexible shafts.

QUICK TIP: Choosing the right shaft flex

Aim for the correct balance between distance and accuracy. The shaft can be made to bend most at a low flex point, i.e. nearer the club head, so you hit the ball higher. Most learners are better with a low flex point as it encourages them to get the ball airborne. A high flex point, nearer the grip of the club, tends to produce a lower ball flight.

SWING WEIGHTS

These are measured in scales from A to D and within each letter from 0–9 (lightest to heaviest). Ignore the A and B scales: they are ultra light. The standard range for ladies is C4–C7; for men, D0–D2. A set of clubs should be matched for swing weight. Your choice will be influenced more by your swing speed than physical strength. A fast swing needs extra club head weight or it may become too fast.

Shaft flex

The weight of the club head will influence the shaft flex. A standard, regular shaft will flex more with a

heavy club head than a light one. The length of the shaft also affects the swing weight: if you're short and need a shorter than standard shaft it will make the swing weight lighter unless some other adjustments are made; self-adhesive lead tape is available for this purpose.

A range of shafts (from left to right): flex twist carbon, boron tipped carbon, normal carbon and a lightweight steel shaft.

PITCHING AND SAND WEDGES

The pitching wedge has a flat, narrow sole and straight leading edge, encouraging a crisp contact with the ball even from a hard, bare lie. The sand wedge sole is heavier and more rounded, and the back edge of the sole is lower than the front leading edge. This helps the club to bounce through the sand and not dig in too deeply, which a pitching wedge tends to do. The sand wedge is the heaviest in a set, and it encourages the club to keep on moving through the sand and the ball.

Notice the space under the front edge of the sand wedge (left); it sits on the flange at the back of the sole. The pitching wedge has a flat sole, so the leading front edge can be on the ground.

QUICK TIP: Playing from grass

The sand wedge may be used from grass as well as bunkers, but you'll need some soft grass underneath the ball. Don't use it from a hard, bare lie as its sole will tend to bounce.

PUTTERS

Choosing the right putter is an extremely personal decision as there are so many designs available, ranging from traditional shapes to some ultra modern ones. There are no simple rules; you just have to find the one that works best for you. If you can get the ball in the hole and are confident with any design of putter, then use it.

This is the golf club you will use most in a round and is therefore perhaps the most important one in your bag. Most established golfers have spare putters because the old faithful will misbehave occasionally; this is the time for a change, even for a short period. Then when you return to your favourite again, it will feel a lot better.

Putter shaft lengths

These vary from 80cm (32in) to 90cm (36in), so shaft length is worth considering if you happen to be tall or short. However, a shorter shaft will make the head weight feel lighter, and a longer shaft increases the feel of the head weight. It is always a good idea to choose a putter

These three putter heads show varying degrees of offset, which is designed to position your hands forward of the striking face. From the left: no offset; $1/4$ inch offset; and $1/2$ inch offset.

with a lie angle that allows you to keep the sole flat, and you should stand with your eye line over the ball.

Grip thickness

This is determined by the size of your hands and length of your fingers. Ladies' grips are the thinnest ones, and Jumbo grips the thickest. Aim to have the fingers of your left hand just touching the fleshy part of your thumb joint when they are closed around the grip. The right hand can then hold the grip in the fingers and fall with the fleshy part of the right thumb joint on top of the left thumb.

Find the correct grip thickness: the finger should just meet the fleshy part of the thumb joint (centre). The thumb joint overlapping the fingers (left) or a space (right) is unsuitable.

QUICK TIP: The right thickness

Too thin a grip causes the fingertips to dig into your palm, but too thick a grip won't allow your fingers to close properly around it. Make sure that he grip of your putter is right for you.

STARTING TO PLAY

Before you rush straight to the course and expect to be able to play golf, take time to learn the correct basic skills on a driving range or practice ground with a pro.

SEEK OUT A PRO

Many beginners have tried playing a few rounds of golf with a friend, then realized that it is not as easy as they thought. When they finally seek the services of a golf professional, many faults have to be undone before the correct fundamentals of technique can be introduced.

Choose a teacher who is prepared to teach you from scratch. Some professionals specialize in specific areas of the game and may not teach beginners. Try to find one who inspires you with confidence and with whom you can establish a rapport. Don't be afraid to ask for advice on all aspects of the game.

WHAT SORT OF LESSONS?

When you book your lessons, try to get your first ones closely grouped – perhaps one or two per week to help you build a consistent set up and basic swing, so you hit the ball with a degree of reliability before you attempt playing a round of golf.

QUICK TIP: Always warm up first

Get into a routine of warming up before you play, especially on cold days when a small strain could seriously affect your swing. Do some loosening exercises to stretch out your muscles and hit 20 or so practice balls with different clubs.

Practise as much as you can between lessons to train your golf muscles. Learning a good swing is just as important an investment as the equipment you buy, so allocate a large percentage of your financial outlay to tuition and, if necessary, economize on your clubs. Don't take the cheapest lessons – they will not be very good.

Group tuition

This is an inexpensive way of getting started. Many pros run evening classes but you will share the teacher with others. If you can afford it, a one-to-one relationship or learning in a smaller group will help you to progress faster.

You can't learn all you need to know about playing golf from a book, so take lessons from your local professional.

Be patient

Golf cannot be learned in a weekend, and as long as you play you can still improve if you are reasonably fit. There's no limit to the number of lessons you can take, whatever your ability and experience. Even top pros take lessons from their favourite golfing gurus.

PRACTICE

Regular practice will tell your brain how to organize the movements of your body. To practise constructively, you must have the right thoughts in your mind. Here are some useful tips and guidelines to help you.

Set yourself goals

Golf is a target game, so practice should always include targets. Make your practice as similar as possible to the real thing, especially the swing. Your aim and alignment are crucial factors; if they are not correct, your swing will compensate with faults. Check that your thoughts and reality correspond by placing some clubs on the ground to check your feet, club face and ball positions.

QUICK TIP: Be positive in practice

Just aimlessly hitting balls on the practice ground or the driving range is nothing more than mere physical exercise; it will not improve your game and may do damage.

Once you have a target and aim in mind, try to visualize the shot you are practising. Imagine the flight the ball will take. How high is the flight? Where will the ball land? How much roll will it have? Set yourself competitive goals, such as hitting seven out of ten bunker shots on to the green, or eight out of ten drives between two target trees. Play some chips and putts from different positions around the green; see how many times you can get down in two.

Vary your shots

Never practise hitting the ball flat out with any club. To promote control and feel, practise half- and three-quarter shots, then hit two different lofted clubs the same distance. You will soon realize the distance that can be achieved with little effort. Do not always practise with the same clubs, but try to introduce lots of variation.

In practice, when setting up for a shot, lay some clubs on the ground through which to swing at your target.

THE SET UP

Golf is a game of repetition. It demands a good routine to bring about the consistency of shots that is required to keep your scores low out on the course. That routine starts with the correct set up, which is the foundation of a sound, rhythmic swing.

FIVE PARTS OF THE SET UP

If your set up is good, all the subsequent actions in the golf swing are more likely to be simple and successful. It is all too easy to rush through this first part and then gallop on to what is often seen as the business end of golf – hitting the ball. However, do not allow yourself to fall into this trap.

QUICK TIP: Train your body and mind

Learning to play golf is essentially a training process, which is not as physically demanding as, say, soccer or tennis, but as skilled as playing a musical instrument. It will take time to train your mind to control your muscles in a new way. Knowing how to move is not enough – to be consistent and improve your scores, you must practise basic moves and exercises until they are ingrained and you can repeat them without thinking about what you are doing, automatically and instinctively.

A good set up is an intrinsic part of your routine when you are preparing to take a shot. If it is done correctly, a good stroke is more likely.

The set up consists of all the things you must do before you take a swing. It can be separated into five distinct parts in the order in which they occur:

1 Aim: align your club to the target.

2 Grip: place your hands on the club.

3 Ball position: position your body in relation to the ball.

4 Body alignment: align your body to the target.

5 Posture: position your body for the shot.

QUICK TIP: Work around your body

As you deal with all the parts of the set up that are listed above, it is very important to keep working around your natural body movements. You will keep referring to these throughout the swing-building process featured in the next chapter (see page 30).

AIM

The part of the club you aim with is the bottom front edge, called the 'leading edge'. You must establish a right-angled (90 degrees) relationship between the edge and your target line in order to aim the club correctly. To do this, prepare your shot in the following way every time. This is the beginning of your routine.

Ball-to-target-line

Start by standing directly behind your ball, facing your target and looking over the ball towards the target. Establish an imaginary line from the middle of your ball to the middle of your target. This line is called the

Using a forward marker, you should aim your club correctly at your intended target.

The shoulders, waist, feet and club head should all be square to the target line.

'ball-to-target line'. As your target will normally be a reasonable distance away from you, and it will be difficult to keep a good fix on it as you move to take up your position at the ball, you will find it helps to pick out something on your ball-to-target line to aim your shot over. This is called your 'forward marker' – it could be a leaf, an old divot, a twig or a broken tee – anything you can see clearly. You will find it much easier to aim over your forward marker two to three yards away than towards a target 200 yards in the distance.

You should now find it reasonably easy to walk towards your ball and then place the leading edge of your club at 90 degrees to your ball-to-target line. You have achieved the correct aim.

QUICK TIP: Aiming the club

The correct aim of the golf club is when you can establish a 90-degree relationship between the leading edge and the ball-to-target line, i.e. the imaginary line running from the middle of the ball to the middle of the target.

GRIP

The grip refers to the position of your hands on the handle of the club, not the strength with which you grasp it. When you perfect your grip, you will feel as though the club has become almost an extension of your arms and body which you can 'feel' throughout your golf swing.

A natural position

If you are holding the club correctly, it will become an extension of your hands and arms, and whatever your hands do will be reflected and extended by the club. The grip you choose will depend on several factors, such as your age, strength and the size of your hands. You need to develop a good grip as it controls the way in which your hands help generate club head speed in your swing and this, in turn, affects the distance you hit the ball. The swing path of the club head is also influenced by your grip, determining whether or not the club face will be square at impact and whether the ball will fly straight. Building a good grip will make hitting a ball much easier.

Types of grip

There are several grips that golfers use, ranging from the overlapping, or Vardon, grip to the interlocking and baseball grips. You should select the one that suits you best but it is important that both your hands work

The left-hand line, or 'V', should point up to the right shoulder from the left thumb and left side of the palm.

together in unison when you are taking a shot. The overlapping grip is the most popular and is suitable for those golfers with large or average size hands (see pages 22–23 for how to build this type of grip), whereas the interlocking grip is better suited to people with short fingers as it links the hands together (ask your pro to show you). Beginners may start off with a 'two-handed' baseball grip because it is the easiest, most natural way to grip a club, but if you want to achieve maximum distance it is better to adopt another grip such as the one shown overleaf.

QUICK TIP: Grip key facts

● The aim of the grip is to establish the placing of your hands on the club by the method shown overleaf.
● You should also achieve a good degree of comfort in the correct holding position.

1 Overlapping grip: lay the club in the mid-knuckle point of the left hand. The ridge at the back of the grip will drop into it. Wrap the fingers of the left hand around the grip of the club.

2 Wrap the upper part of the left hand around the shaft of the club so that the left pad wraps over the grip and clasps it. Place the left thumb pointing down the top right-hand quarter of the grip with the 'V' in line with the right shoulder.

3 Now place the club in the mid-knuckle point of the right hand and then move it up the grip towards the left hand as illustrated in the photographs above.

4 Now overlap or interlock the little finger of the right hand with the index finger of the left hand. The lifeline of the left hand should cover the left thumb from top to bottom. The right thumb creates a 'V' or line with the right shoulder.

BALL POSITION

The ball must be positioned in the forward half of the stance (halfway between the centre of your feet and your front foot) for all normal shots. This makes the back of the ball available for you to strike, and places you in a position where you will be encouraged to use your body weight correctly through the swing.

To establish the correct ball position, stand with your feet together (left). Move your left foot into the correct position in relation to the ball (centre), and then establish the stance width by moving your right foot (right).

Make sure that your feet are parallel to the target line with the ball positioned forward in your stance, as is shown by these golf clubs laid out on the ground.

The ball should be positioned in the middle of your stance, forwards in the hitting zone.

BODY ALIGNMENT

You must position your body in relation to your target. You should align your toes, knees, hips and shoulders parallel to the ball-to-target line. This ensures that your swing will direct the ball towards the target.

Practice drill

Place two clubs on the ground, one running parallel to your ball-to-target line and one at right angles to it. They should make a 'T' shape and there should be a gap of about 30cm (12in) between them. Face the

shaft, which is running parallel with your ball-to-target line, making sure that your toes, knees,

It is very important to position your shoulders parallel to the ball-to-target line, so it makes sense to keep your toes, knees and hips parallel, too.

QUICK TIP: Body position
● The ball should be positioned in the forward half of your stance, somewhere between the centre and the left heel.
● Your toes, knees, hips and shoulders should be parallel to your ball-to-target line.

hips and shoulders are all parallel to it. Use the other shaft running back between your feet to indicate the position of the ball, and make sure that this is halfway between the centre of your feet and your left foot. This is the ideal position for a medium iron.

You will find any lines placed on the ground parallel to your target line a great help during practice.

POSTURE

This is the positioning of your body at set up. Good posture is very important as it will establish a stable, balanced position from which you can move freely; the correct distance between you and the ball; and the correct angle of swing to produce a solid strike on the back of the ball.

The golf swing is an athletic movement involving practically every part of your body. The posture position is the final link in your set up and must place you in readiness for that free athletic movement.

Good posture is the key to balanced movement and an effective golf swing. Keep your chin up (left) away from your torso and your back straight (right).

The correct posture: bend forward from your hips until the club touches the ground, then flex your knees.

QUICK TIP: Why you need good posture

● To establish a position that will give you the opportunity to move freely and to remain balanced during your swing.

● To establish the correct distance between you and the ball.

● To establish the correct angle of swing.

THE SWING

Having established the correct set up, you are now ready to swing the golf club itself. The purpose of your swing is to generate power, but many new, untrained golfers hurl themselves around so much in an attempt to do this that they have little chance of hitting the ball properly, far less sending it in the correct direction. This is quite natural.

ACCURACY AND CONTROL

When you stand on a teeing ground for the first time and look down the fairway, what is the first thing in your mind? Usually, how far away the

To achieve distance from a good shot, think about your target and where you want the ball to land.

flag seems. The next question is usually: 'How do I manage to hit the ball that far?' Most beginners think, erroneously, that the answer is to hit it really hard.

So, without the proper training, it is very easy for you, as a new golfer, to fall into the bad habit of trying to hit the ball much too hard. However, this will just make it difficult to control any of the actions that you are trying to make. Power has taken over and any accuracy and control could well be lost for ever. You should not let this happen to you.

Achieving distance

You will achieve far more distance from a ball struck well with less power than from a ball that is struck badly but with more power. Take your time and never force a shot in an attempt just to hit it further. Always think of hitting the ball better, not harder!

QUICK TIP: Co-ordinate your movement

To swing the club well means that you will generate power whilst giving yourself a reasonable opportunity to strike the ball accurately and send it in the correct direction. This demands a well balanced, co-ordinated movement marrying together the two areas of power generation: your body action, and the areas you will be working on, firstly to understand them and then train yourself to put them into practice.

BODY ACTION

It is essential that you use your body correctly if you want to build a good swing. It is the biggest source of power in the swing, and how it moves will influence how well you are able to swing your arms, hands and club.

The pivoting motion

Your body action determines how you use your large muscles; how much power you generate; how your arms, hands and golf club combine to create an effective swing; and its pace. You'll need a good pivoting motion as well as the correct weight transfer during your swing. The pivoting action of your body helps return the club head consistently to the ball. Together with your weight transfer, it will generate the power needed to hit the ball the distance you require.

A good pivoting action will help you to generate power in your golf swing.

Try to practise your pivoting motion without a club, as shown above. You can do this standing on the practice ground or you may find it helpful to do so in front of a mirror.

QUICK TIP: Right and left sides

Think about your body pivot when you swing. Your body will pivot and move your weight into your right side during the backswing. Then your body will pivot into and around your left side, transferring your weight, through impact, on to your left foot by the end of your swing.

Backswing pivot

As your body starts to turn, your weight shifts on to
your right foot, moving more into your right side. Keep
the flex in your right knee constant, so that your weight
stays directly above your right foot. Your shoulders
should have turned over 90 degrees from the starting
position. Your hips should have turned 30–40 degrees,
and 75 per cent of your body weight should now be
over your right foot.

Don't keep your head too still, but let it turn a little to
the right. At the end of the backswing, your right thigh
and the left side of your back should feel a little tense;
this is indicative of the power that is stored up ready
to use when striking the ball.

The downswing

Move the whole of your left side smoothly across until
50 per cent of your weight is on your left foot. Start
turning your upper left side behind you, bringing more
your weight on to your left foot as the pivot continues.

QUICK TIP: Body action key points
- Maintain your balance throughout the swing.
- Maintain the spinal angle throughout the swing.
- Control your weight transfer smoothly.
- Create controlled power.
- Control the speed of the swing.

Your right side will be pulled through by the movement of your left. At the end of the swing, your right shoulder will be closer to the target than your left, your hips will be at 90 degrees to the ball-to-target line, and 90 per cent of your weight will be over your left foot with only the toe of your right foot on the ground. Your head should finish looking down the target line. Throughout the swing, the angle of your spine, created at set up, should stay constant.

Practising the pivoting action helps you to develop the feel of the golf swing. You need to focus on achieving a 90-degree pivot back and through. Notice from the photographs above how this affects your weight transfer and balance. You should maintain a constant spine angle throughout.

THE BACKSWING

Now the time has arrived to look at the swing in detail and to analyze all the different parts in detail, so that you can learn how to build a good, consistent swing. The first part of the movement – the backswing – is the preparation for the swing itself.

Pre-swing routine

To create an effective swing, you must position both yourself and the ball in the correct direction and in a powerful fashion. If you can complete the backswing correctly, then the forward swing has a good chance of being equally successful. It is always helpful to develop a pre-swing

If your body is in the correct position at the top of the backswing, you are more likely to produce an equally good downswing and follow through and thereby hit a successful shot.

routine. Just before you start swinging the club, there are a couple of helpful movements that you can make: these are the waggle and the forward press.

Waggle

This movement is designed to help prevent you 'freezing' over the ball. It is a good idea to build the waggle into your swing routine in order to help alleviate any tension in your body before swinging the club. A slight movement of the wrists taking the club back and forth on either side of the ball will help to ease the pressure. So before you make your swing, just shift your weight slightly from foot to foot to relax your feet and legs.

Forward press

A smooth takeaway will lead to a more controlled golf swing. Although it does not have to be slow, it must be smooth or in tempo (see the tip below).

QUICK TIP: The speed of the golf swing

This is determined by how long it takes the large muscles to reach the top of the backswing, so if you are aware of arriving at the top you have performed the swing at a speed you can control. This allows you to find your own tempo. It does not matter if your tempo is quick, medium or slow – it is the swing that controls the rhythm.

Encourage a smooth swing with a slight forward movement of the hands and wrists, leaving the club head on the ground behind the ball to create a recoil and trigger the backswing. Alternatively, try a slight 'kicking in' of the right knee, again creating the recoil. If you find it difficult to get started in the backswing, you should spend some time experimenting with both systems and select the one that works best for you.

Achieving direction and power

A successful golf shot requires two elements: direction and power. Look in detail at the movements you have to make to encourage both of these things to happen, so you can build a routine that will eventually lead to a consistent swing. It is advisable to start off with a 6 or 7 iron. These clubs will make the ball travel far enough to let you see what you have achieved. They are not power clubs, which are designed to send the ball a long way, so there is no pressure on you to hit the ball really hard or smash the living daylights out of it.

QUICK TIP: Shoulder turn

If, at waist level, you discover that your shoulders have not turned enough, then you have taken the club head to the far side of the ball-to-target line. This often happens when the club has been picked up or lifted by the wrists or a bending of the elbows.

The takeaway

In the takeaway, the club is taken straight back from the ball, close to the ground, for the first 12–15cm (5–6in). The club head will be on the target line parallel to the shoulders. You should feel the club head, shaft, left hand, arm and shoulder moving as one unit.

Waist level may sometimes be referred to as a 'half swing', where the shoulders have turned through

Weight transfer is a very important factor in your golf swing. It mimics a throwing action where your weight is transferred from one side of the body to the other as you swing through the strike: weight back, weight through.

approximately 45 degrees. If you were aligned correctly in the set up (see page 26), and you are in this position, then you should achieve good direction. You are on target to make a good swing and hit the ball correctly.

The second half

You complete the backswing by turning until your left shoulder is between your chin and the ball. Your shoulders will have turned through approximately 90 degrees. Your weight will be over the right hip, knee and ankle. You will feel some torsion around the hips and the inside of the left leg, and your hips will have rotated 45 degrees.

Coiling

Releasing this coiled tension will produce the hit. You may lift your left heel off the ground if wished. Your shoulders and legs have been fully used, and this spring-like effect is now ready to 'explode' into action (see opposite) on the downswing.

QUICK TIP: At waist level

● The leading edge of the club head will be at right angles to the shoulders.

● The number of knuckles visible on the back of the left hand will be the same as in the set up.

● If your shoulders have turned in advance of the hands, the club head has been brought inside the line too quickly.

THE DOWNSWING

Initiate this with your legs. Transferring the weight to the left leg will start the club moving downwards on the correct inside attack. The hands and arms will then take over to deliver the club head back to the ball.

Delivering the club head

The wrists uncock while the arms swing the club down. Your left arm maintains its firmness, giving your swing a good arc width and building up club head speed to hit the ball a long way. As your right arm starts to straighten, it generates more club head speed. Meanwhile, from the top of the backswing, your raised left foot will lower itself to the ground. Both feet will stay there throughout impact with the ball – the foundation of a smooth, solid swing. Keep your balance; if you lose it, you're trying too hard. As you swing down, the speed of the downswing will get gradually faster until the wrists start to uncock, delivering the club head to the ball at tremendous speed.

QUICK TIP: Cocked wrists

At the top of the backswing, your wrists will be hinged, (cocked). This is caused at waist level by the weight of the club head and momentum of the swing. Your left arm should be comfortably straight. It should not buckle under pressure. The club shaft should be parallel to the ball-to-target line, aiming slightly to the left.

As the club descends, ther speed of the downswing increases, the wrists uncock and the club head impacts the ball at tremendous speed.

IMPACT

At the moment of impact, the left side of your body will turn fractionally to the left. However, you will not achieve maximum club head speed until both your arms become straight just after contact with the ball to give maximum power through the hit.

Making good contact

Your posture at impact should mirror what it was at address (see pages 28–29). You should not try to lift the ball or scoop it up – the club's loft will do this for you.

The way the club face strikes the ball is very important, so focus on producing the right contact. You should aim to swing the club head through a circle from the top of the backswing, brushing the ground at the exact spot where the ball is sitting. Remember that a good-looking swing is no good at all unless contact with the ball is accurate, producing a good shot.

KEEP IT TOGETHER

Remember that your feet should stay in contact with the ground throughout impact, giving your swing a solid foundation. Your whole body is working together as one to hit the ball as hard as you can. You must not allow any one part of your body to become dominant. Just focus on what you are doing.

Contact is made with the ball at the bottom of the swing, using the loft of the club to lift the ball naturally.

QUICK TIP: Contact

● With medium and short irons, contact with the ball should occur just before the bottom of the swing.

● With long irons and fairway woods, contact should be at the bottom of the swing.

● With a driver, you should strike the ball slightly on the upswing.

THE FOLLOW THROUGH

From impact, the club will continue to swing freely through the swing plane until it comes to a halt with the shaft behind your head at the top of the follow through. You should be in a well-balanced position.

After impact

Your body turns to the left together with the club face and the path of your swing. The left arm bends downwards slightly and your right shoulder comes through under your chin. This helps keep the swing on a wide arc through the hitting area and high into the follow through. Your body turns fully to the left and your chest and hips should face the target as you finish.

A balanced finish

To free the swing to carry on to an even higher finish, your head should rise naturally as your right shoulder hits your chin. Your right foot is pulled up on to the toes

QUICK TIP: Swing guide

● There should not be any independent movement in your arms and hands.

● The plane of the swing is the key to striking the ball consistently and correctly.

● Your arms and hands should keep moving on the swing plane throughout.

due to the right side pulling up through the follow through. It is very important to maintain tempo and achieve a balanced finish with good control of the club.

THE LONG GAME

You will gain great satisfaction from developing a sound long game and hitting accurate shots with a wood or long iron, but first you need to learn how to produce a consistently reliable swing in order to master the longer-shafted, straighter-faced clubs, which are more difficult to control than medium irons.

WOODS AND LONG IRONS

Your longer clubs are designed to develop more momentum and thereby send the ball further even though you keep your swing the same as for the mid irons. The only adjustments you need make are to your set up and stance. Do not be tempted to force these shots. All you need to do is to make some minor

QUICK TIP: Types of clubs

Golf clubs can be split into the three following groups:

- The medium irons (5, 6 and 7)
- The woods and long irons
- The short irons.

The woods and long irons consist of all the woods and the 1, 2, 3 and 4 irons. The short irons are the 8, 9, pitching wedge and sand iron. At this stage, don't even think of using a 1 or 2 wood or 1 or 2 iron. These are the most difficult clubs.

modifications for the club you are using and then to swing it as you have already learned.

Adjust your stance

Woods and long irons have longer shafts and create more momentum; hence, they require a more stable stance than for your medium irons to maintain your stability and balance. The length of shaft also affects the arc of your swing, making it slightly shallower.

Therefore you need to create a more sweeping type of strike. To take all this into account, you will need to widen your stance fractionally and adjust the ball position. However, do remember that this will change your weight distribution at set up.

Stand with your feet apart so that if you drew a line down from the inside of each arm it would then extend to the inside of each foot. You should position the ball opposite the inside of your left heel. This will have the effect of your weight distribution being 55 per cent on your right foot and 45 per cent on your left foot.

QUICK TIP: Your stance
● Medium irons: the middle of each foot should be under the inside of each arm.
● Long irons: your stance is as above but slightly wider.
● Short irons: your stance should be narrower.

When hitting a shot with your longer clubs, you will need to produce a sweeping swing to make the ball fly further. Keep it smooth and unhurried – you don't have to hit the ball harder to make it travel a long way.

QUICK TIP: Practise your set up and swing

Now that you have made all the necessary changes to your stance, you should follow your normal set-up routine and practise swinging the club from this slightly different position. Always follow your full set-up drill and you will soon get used to the small changes that are required to use the longer clubs. You will start to make them automatically without even having to think about what you are doing.

Follow through with your wood – you should feel your weight transferring from your right to your left side.

QUICK TIP: Swing slowly

Many golfers swing too hard with their long clubs, trying to hit the ball over super-human distances. However, because the shaft is longer and the club head travels on a bigger arc, you will need to make a slower swing. A smooth, unhurried one is always the best swing.

SHORT IRONS

These clubs are specially designed to give the ball a high floating style of flight, so that it will stop more quickly on the green. Because they have a shorter shaft, they will not send the ball as far as your mid irons. You should use them to play shorter, more lofted shots, such as out of the rough.

Your stance

Narrow the width of your stance, so an imaginary line extending down from the inside of each arm ends on the outside of each foot. This provides the correct stability and mobility for your short shots. You should feel slightly more weight on your left foot. Try to aim for a weight distribution of 55 per cent on your left foot and 45 per cent on your right. This will give you the correct angle of swing.

The set up

Now set up in the usual way; adjusting your width of stance and weight distribution are all that are needed. Make sure that you check your posture and swing in the normal way for an iron shot.

QUICK TIP: Less mobility

Note that the narrower stance means that your body is less mobile for the short iron shots.

FAIRWAY WOODS

The fairway woods, which include the 3, 4, 5, 7 and 9 woods, are more lofted and easier to use than the straighter-faced long irons, making them increasingly popular with golfers of all abilities and handicaps.

The set up

The wide sole of the club should sit flat on the ground with the ball positioned opposite your left heel and your hands level or just slightly behind the back of the ball. This adjustment to your usual set up, when combined with the long shaft of the club, helps you to produce a sweeping arc of contact on the ball rather than the more downward contact you create with an iron.

It is better to use fairway woods when playing from the semi-rough as they can sweep more easily and cleanly through the grass than a long iron club.

To check your set up, ground your fairway wood on a hard, flat surface with the club face aiming down the target line (see the photographs below). Check the angle of the shaft. Hold the club lightly in the fingers of one hand; don't grip it. Start building your stance around the club and take your grip.

Wind conditions

These should be considered before selecting a fairway wood as opposed to a long iron. A 5 wood, for example, will tend to flight the ball on a higher trajectory than a 2 or 3 iron. When playing into a strong wind, play a long iron to prevent the ball travelling too high into the air.

The sole of the wood is sitting flat in the correct position (left). Note the angle of the shaft. The incorrect way to ground a wood is shown (right). The back edge is up and the loft on the face has been reduced to zero.

Playing in semi-rough

Your fairway woods are useful where the grass is longer in the semi-rough. They will tend to sweep cleanly through the grass whereas it may grab and twist a long iron club. However, you should always be cautious if the ball is sitting down really low in the grass. Sometimes it is better to stay safe and be less ambitious. Rather than try and hit any long club, the safe percentage shot would be a lofted short iron club.

If the ball is nestling low down in the grass, you can hit it with a fairway wood or choose to play safe and use a more lofted short iron.

QUICK TIP: Striking the ball cleanly

It is safe to use a fairway wood if the club can contact the ball below its equator. This makes it suitable for hitting from most reasonably good grassy lies just off the fairway. To strike the ball cleanly, contact must occur at the bottom of the swing.

When using woods, try to hit the ball with a descending blow which flattens out just before the bottom of the swing arc. Try to think of it as a sweeping action.

QUICK TIP: You need a good lie

You must be able to strike the ball below its equator if you are to use a wood. To use a 3 wood from the fairway, you will need a good lie with the whole of the ball sitting above the turf.

USING THE RIGHT CLUBS

You don't have to learn a different swing for each club, but the distance you stand from the ball and where you position it in your stance will need to be adjusted according to the length and design of the club you use. Shots with long irons and woods are more difficult, so practise to achieve consistency and accuracy. Start off with medium clubs and progress to longer ones.

Selecting the right club

There are a number of specific factors that you need to consider before you finally select the right club for each golf shot. Read through the following guidelines to choosing the right club.

- Consider wind direction and strength: may be strong on exposed courses.
- Temperature: a warm ball travels up to 20 yards further than a cold ball.
- Ground firmness: will the ball stop quickly or run, and if so how much?
- A backdrop of trees or a bank behind the green will have a tendency to make it look much closer to you than it really is.

Club/yardage chart

Yards	Irons	Woods
110	PW	-
120	9	-
130	8	-
140	7	-
150	6	-
160	5	-
170	4	-
180	3	5
190	2	4
210	-	3
225	-	2
240	-	1

- If there is no background behind the green, there will be a tendency to give the impression that it is further than it is.
- The size of the green: large greens will look closer whereas small greens will look further away than they actually are.
- The length of the flagsticks have a similar visual effect: long ones will look closer whereas short ones will look further away.
- There may be 'dead ground', especially if you are playing over mounds.
- Work on knowing the distance you can hit each club.

JUDGING DISTANCE

In order to select the correct club to hit the ball to the target, you need to be able to judge the distance that it needs to travel. You should know, within 10 yards, how far you can hit each club.

Practice drill

Gather together about 20 balls of the same make, the type you would normally use for playing. On the

QUICK TIP: Expect mishits

When you are starting out, expect some mishits that do not fly far enough, but you should always choose a club on the basis that you will hit a good shot.

practice ground, hit all the balls with a mid iron (say, a 6 or 7 iron) and then pace out the distance to the spot where a group of good shots have landed. If you make your strides a yard each in length, then you can calculate how far you hit with that iron. Now repeat the exercise with each of your other irons. There should be approximately 10 yards between each club. If your 6 iron goes 150 yards, a 7 iron should go 140 yards, and a 5 iron 160 yards. You will need to use your irons for the

Instead of rushing your shot, do take your time to look at your target and work out the distance the ball must fly in order to reach it.

You may find it useful to stand to the side of your intended line and, in your mind, divide the distance the ball must fly into two or three equidistant parts.

accurate approach shots, whereas your woods are the distance clubs. They will have a greater differential with about 20 yards between clubs.

Yardage charts

Most golf courses issue a pre-measured course planner showing the distance to the centre or the front of each green, although you will find that it is always wise to check this measurement out for yourself.

Split the distance down

Before playing a shot, always stand slightly to the side in order to try and estimate the distance between you and your target. You will find that this is much easier than judging it from behind the ball.

Now split the distance down into two or three sections, so that you can visualize a 50-yard mark, followed by another 50-yard mark. By adding these figures together, it is possible for you to build up a more accurate picture rather than just looking from behind the ball straight at the target.

QUICK TIP: Wind direction

To judge the wind direction, you should do the following:

● First, look at the flag. Is it moving?
● Next, take a look at the tree tops.
● Lastly, hold up a handkerchief and observe what happens.

YOUR TARGET CLUBS

The medium irons – the 5, 6 and 7 irons – are the target clubs which are normally used for approaching the green from about 130–170 yards away. You should never hit a ball flat out with a medium iron. Before making your final choice of club, try to assess the flag position and whether more trouble lies in front of or behind the green.

Set up for medium irons

For your set up, position the ball 7–10cm (3–4in) inside the left heel with your hands slightly forward of the ball so that the club shaft and your left arm are in line (looking from the front, not the side). For the grip for medium irons, you should position your hands normally with 4cm (1$\frac{1}{2}$in) showing at the top of the grip.

Playing in the wind

Always use the wind to your advantage rather than fight it. If you are playing into a left-to-right wind, don't try and draw the shot. Instead, set up to allow for the wind and then play a normal straight shot which the wind will move back to the target. You need to visualize your target – in this case, left of its actual position – and then you should swing towards your imagined target.

When you are playing into or across the wind, you should always use a larger club than normal. Make sure that you swing a little shorter and do not force it.

In the set up, the ball is inside the left heel. The left arm and club shaft are in line (right). Position your hands normally on the grip (above) with 4cm (1^1/$_2$in) showing at the top.

When playing into the wind, choke down the grip, leaving 7–10cm (3–4in) showing at the top. Use this grip when you play low punch shots, half shots and recoveries from trees.

A wider stance will help maintain balance and restrict the amount of body turn and length of the swing. Use the same principles as when you are playing a low shot.

Bad lies

If you hit an off-line tee shot which lands in a bad lie, the medium irons are good for playing back on to the fairway. The best club to use when the ball is down in thick rough and you can only see the top is a 7 iron. This is because the shorter shaft gives a steeper swing, and there is sufficient loft to get the ball airborne with forward movement.

When playing from a bad lie with too much grass between the club face and ball, use a middle to short club rather than a long iron or a wood.

DEALING WITH HAZARDS

There are many situations on a golf course that are hazardous, but the only things that are classified as hazards are sand and water. Trees, the rough, uneven lies, grass hollows and banks are featured here because you will encounter these obstacles and will need to modify your normal swing in order to pull off a special shot that will help you recover from an awkward position.

IN THE ROUGH

If your ball ends up in the rough, you must decide whether the lie is so severe that it prevents you playing a club long enough to reach the green. If this is the case, do not take risks; play a safety shot out to the middle of the fairway.

The ball is sitting down, or plugged, and direct club to ball contact is impossible. Use a lofted club and hit down into the ground and the ball.

QUICK TIP: Take a risk or play safe?

Beginners often hit their ball into trouble and are then tempted to go for a miracle recovery shot. Although they may succeed gloriously 10 per cent of the time, the other 90 per cent they will end up in worse trouble. You must learn when to take a calculated risk and when to play safe.

Texture

The texture of the rough will affect the club head in numerous ways as you swing through it. Be aware that there will be more resistance and a tendency to twist as the club head contacts the rough and the ball. Allow for this by making your grip firmer than usual, especially in the top three fingers of your left hand. The rough will grab the hosel of the club, causing the club face to close at impact and the ball to fly left of your target. To allow for this, you should aim 10–15 yards right of your target with both the club face and your feet.

Lower ball flight

The club face will not make direct contact with the ball, and some grass will be trapped between the two, creating a cushioning effect and making the ball respond differently. It will tend to fly lower and shoot forwards with loss of control and without any backspin on landing. You can allow for this by taking a more lofted club than usual and playing the ball further towards your right foot. This will have the effect of producing a steeper downward angle of attack on the ball which has more chance of success. There is a risk that the club head will turn over at impact and smother the shot as the hosel and shaft become entangled in the grass, but your firmer grip and open club face at address should help to prevent this happening.

Ball sitting up high

Occasionally, the ball will sit up high on top of the rough and then you can use a straighter-faced club,

QUICK TIP: Different lies in the rough

You need to be able to recognize the following different lies in the rough in order to use the correct golf technique when you are tackling each one.

● **Good lie:** This is easy to spot, but you must take care to observe which way the grass is growing. If it lies in the same direction as you are going to swing, it is a good lie. It may be better to use a wood than a long iron as it will slide easily through long grass.

● **Normal lie:** You can see the ball but it is low down in longish grass, which will get between your club face and the ball at impact. A wood may be better but if you use an iron, increase your grip pressure for better club control.

● **Bad lie:** The ball nestles down very low in long grass, almost obliterated from view. Use a very lofted club, such as a wedge, to drive the club head down and through the ball, lifting it back on to the fairway.

such as a 4 iron. Position the ball to the left in your stance and don't ground your club too hard at address (and risk moving the ball). Take care you do not hit underneath the ball taking the grass below it. Instead, hold the club head in such a way that you address the middle of the ball and produce a sweeping action –avoid a steep downward strike.

When the ball is sitting up, do not press the club head down into the ground.

Ball in heather

This golf shot is always misleading as heather looks short but is actually very tough and wiry to play from. Do not be tempted to risk any kind of long shot, but instead you should take your penalty and then play a lofted 9 iron or a wedge to move the ball back on to the fairway.

When playing from some wiry heather, use a lofted club and a firm grip. Play the shot in the same way as you would from the deep rough.

BUNKER SHOTS

Your set up, stance and ball position for bunker shots need adjustment. Shuffle your feet into the sand to give your swing a firm base and test the depth and texture of the surface. Do not ground your club in the sand.

Your set up

Position your feet and body on a line 15-20 degrees left of your target with the ball opposite a spot that is just inside your left heel to encourage a steeper swing path travelling parallel to your body's aim, matching your open club face. Focus on a spot behind the ball and strike the sand 5cm (2in) before the ball so it floats out on a cushion of sand. Follow through with the weight on your left foot.

The set up for bunker shots with the feet shuffled into the sand, just enough to cover the soles of your shoes.

QUICK TIP: Never ground your club

The Rules of golf prohibit you from grounding your club in a hazard. Avoid this by taking your grip on the club before entering a bunker and placing your thumbs down a line slightly to the left of the front of the grip to open the club face.

This set up shows two main faults – the club face is de-lofted and the ball is too far back in the stance.

When addressing the ball in a bunker, open your stance and ensure that the club face is open. You should feel relaxed with the club shaft straight up towards you.

QUICK TIP: The stroke

Hitting good shots out of bunkers will save you strokes, so it is well worth practising and perfecting them. The aim is to create quite a steep 'U'-shaped swing so the club head travels through the sand and out the other side in a long and relaxed follow through. Do not chop at the sand or the ball.

Your swing

Unlike other shots, your hands should not rotate through impact; keep your club face open. You should not feel direct contact with the ball. The cushion of sand between the club face and ball helps you take a long swing, so the ball comes out slowly. Keep your swing speed steady – don't rush it. Regular practice instills confidence in hitting successful shots. You must always be relaxed to hit consistently well.

Your club should strike the sand behind the ball, about the length of a credit card, and travel through to a smooth follow through.

QUICK TIP: Bunker know-how

When taking bunker shots, remember the following points:

- You need an open club face.
- You need an open stance.
- Aim and look at a spot a credit card's length behind the ball.
- Take some sand and follow through to shoulder height.

Opposite: Set up with the feet and body aiming left of target. Make a long swing, taking sand before the ball and keeping the club face open at the bottom of the arc.

Greenside bunkers

Greenside bunkers can be defined as those within reach of the pin in one shot. The height of the bunker lip is important; if necessary, come out of a bunker to the side or even backwards, wherever the lips are not so steep. Your feet and body should aim left of the target. Make a long swing, taking sand

A greenside bunker shot requires an open club face with the ball positioned forward in the stance.

behind the ball and keeping the club face open at the bottom with no hint of stopping at the ball. The arms and club should move to the left of the target with the body facing to the left and a long follow through.

Downhill bunker shots

For these shots, you must set up with an open club face with the ball positioned well back in your stance. Aim to hit a couple of inches behind the ball with your weight more on the left foot, so that your body is at right angles to the slope with the shoulders following

Opposite: For a downhill bunker shot, adopt a wider stance with more hip bend, and an open club face. Make an early wrist break to clear the back lip of the bunker and keep the forward swing low after contact. The ball trajectory will tend to be low.

the lie of the slope. Indeed, your weight should stay on the left leg throughout the swing with no hint of falling back. The loft of your club will be reduced because of the slope, and the club head should follow the contour of the sand with a steeper backswing and lower follow through. Your swing should be shorter for this shot, so that the ball will come out of the bunker on a lower trajectory with run.

Uphill bunker shots

These bunker shots are quite tricky and you must adjust your set up accordingly. Your weight should be more on the right side with your club face less open than for a normal bunker shot. Aim to hit the sand only 1–2cm (1/2–1in) behind the ball and focus your eyes on this spot. Your club head should follow the contour of the sand, and the follow through will swing up more quickly. Take a long forward swing because the ball will pop up higher rather than forwards.

Opposite: For an uphill bunker shot, use an open stance with more weight on the right leg. Aim to take less sand before the ball and let the long forward swing follow the contour of the bunker. The ball will come out naturally with a high trajectory.

GOLF TIP: Be courteous

Don't forget to rake up the marks you have left in the bunker; it's courteous to other golfers.

Long bunker shots

To hit the ball a long way from a fairway bunker, you will need a flat lie without any ridges of sand just behind the ball. When you play this shot, you need a wide, sweeping swing and you must ensure that you take the ball first.

Set up and shot

Shorten down on the grip and address the ball halfway up. Select a club with sufficient loft to clear the bunker face. Don't shuffle your feet into the sand; the sole of the club should be level with the equator of the ball. Your arms and club should create a wide, sweeping arc.

Fairway bunkers

Don't think about the distance to the green. Decide which club you need to clear the lip of the bunker; focus on getting the ball into play in a single shot. In a poor lie, play the shot as in a greenside bunker; in a good lie with the ball sitting up, set up with a normal ball position and make a three-quarter swing. Don't contact with the sand before the ball.

When you set up for a long bunker shot, you must shorten down on the grip.

QUICK TIP: Don't hit too hard

Never try to force a long bunker shot. Bear in mind that if you attempt to hit the ball too hard, it will just result in an inaccurate shot and even higher scores.

The correct backswing for a long bunker shot. Your club should be an extension of your arms as they move together to create a wide, sweeping swing through the ball, not the sand.

Plugged bunker shots

The bottom of the ball is below the level of most of the sand; you need a digging action by the leading edge of the club, to explode the ball out and play the shot.

The set up

How well you play this shot depends on experience; sometimes it is better to take a penalty drop. Practise this shot, with the ball in different positions. You must

QUICK TIP: Wet or dry sand

If the bunker is full of wet, firm sand, you may find you need a sharp-edged 9-iron to cut through the sand and get you out of trouble. For dry, soft sand, use a sand wedge.

close the club face slightly, especially if the ball is well buried – the end of the toe should be pointing at the ball. Your stance should be less open than usual with the ball placed back towards the right foot.

The stance is less open than for a normal bunker shot with the ball back towards the right foot. Do not lean backwards and try to scoop the ball out of a plugged lie. Hit down firmly into the sand, allowing the club to explode the ball out.

The swing

Make a steep takeaway with wrist break to create a steeper descending arc as you jab downwards into the sand and ball, with only 2cm (1in) sand before the ball. The ball will fly much lower than usual from this type of lie and will run on landing so you cannot control this shot effectively but you will have escaped!

The ball position is slightly further back in the stance, causing a steeper backswing.

Ball under the lip of a bunker

If you are confronted with an awkward lie where the ball is close to the overhanging lip of a bunker, you can use the same basic technique as for the other bunker shots. However, you will need extra height and a steep downswing arc if you are to hit the ball cleanly out of the sand back on to the grass.

The set up

When you set up for this type of bunker shot, adopt a slightly more open stance than usual, and position the ball further forward. This will give you extra height and effectively increase the loft of your club face. Keep your eyes focused on a spot in the sand behind the ball – about 5–7cm (2–3in) behind it. Don't focus on the ball or you'll hit it too cleanly and thin it into the lip of the bunker. Concentrate on the right spot in the sand.

Set up with an open stance, the club face well open and the ball position forward in your stance.

The swing

With your weight on the right side, swing the club head up quickly with an early wrist break to the full backswing position. Your left arm will lead the downswing in a sharp downward attack into the sand – about 5–7cm (2–3in) behind the ball.

Throughout the forward swing, make sure you keep the club face open. Your hands and the club should move in unison. As you swing down and through, your weight transfers onto the left foot. Don't worry about lifting the ball and scooping it up out of the sand. Let your club do the work for you.

You may not be able to make a full follow through as it will be restricted by the face of the bunker. Don't worry – the ball will rise quickly out of the bunker on impact and by the time you reach this position it will be long gone; it won't matter if your club hits the bank.

QUICK TIP: Conquering hazards

Once you realize the changes you need to make in your address and swing to play shots from hazards and to avoid obstacles, they will become less fearsome. However, try to master these shots on the practice ground or by playing the course on your own, dropping the ball in awkward places, before you attempt to play them in a match.

Make a quick backswing with an early wrist break, then swing
down at a sharp downward angle into the sand behind the ball.

Do not try to scoop up the ball. The face of the bunker may
prevent your full follow through.

TREES

Getting out of trouble is a part of golf, so don't panic if you are confronted with a tree-lined course or water hazard. Instead of seeing all the places where you don't want to hit the ball, focus on your target and visualize a shot with the ball landing in the right place. Shade out any hazard areas and just picture a perfect shot with the sun shining on your target. Light it up and see yourself hitting it. Banish negative thoughts and blot out the clump of trees that stand in your way to the pin.

Although they may look beautiful, trees are potential hazards, especially if your ball ends up under one. If so, you can hit a low shot from underneath or a shot through a gap in the branches. Judging the ball flight through a gap is obviously very difficult, so it is usually more sensible to go for a low shot.

QUICK TIP: Tree options

If there are some trees between you and the hole, you can try doing one of the following:

- Hit over the trees.
- Play around the right side of them with draw (page 90).
- Play around the left side of them with fade (page 87).

These shots are quite advanced, so most beginners should just play sideways, even if it means adding a shot, and then get back into play when you can see the target again.

Playing a low shot

Choose a relatively straight-faced club for this shot. The ball should be back in your stance opposite the mid point between your feet. Try not to hit the ball too hard; if you hit it softly, it will not have the opportunity to rise. You want to keep the ball flight low underneath the branches of the tree, so maintain your swing rhythm and keep your downswing very slow to make good contact with the ball.

Two views of the address position for playing a low shot. To keep the ball flight low, position the ball further back in the stance as shown.

THE FADE

By learning how to shape your shots, you can play them around trees and hazards. The fade is an advanced shot but, with practice, you can master it and it will help get you out of some tricky situations around the course.

Line of ball flight

Use the fade to move the ball from left to right but, before attempting it, stand behind the ball and visualize your shot, choosing the line on which you want the ball to start. Build your stance and alignment around this line because the swing path direction is the most powerful force and dictates where the ball flies initially.

Club selection and set up

To impart clockwise spin on the ball and make it bend to the right, you need to select a straight-faced club.

QUICK TIP: Fade or draw?

How do you decide when you should play a left-to-right shot (a fade) or a right-to-left shot (a draw)? The following advice may well help you to avoid playing the wrong shot at the wrong time.

- If you have a tight lie, play a fade.
- If the lie is good, you can play a draw.
- Never try to fade the short irons.
- It is easier to fade with a straighter club.

A 4 or 5 iron is usually best for this. When you set up for this shot, aim to the left with the ball positioned just inside your left heel. For the grip, place both thumbs down on the grip just left of the centre line. When you look down, you should see less of the back of your left hand, and more of the back of your right hand than you would do with a normal shot.

In the set up (above and below), aim to the left with the ball inside the left heel. Adjust your grip for an open club face through impact.

QUICK TIP: Don't rush

Don't be tempted to rush this shot; just approach it in a calm, considered way and make sure you take a smooth, slow swing.

The swing

You need a steep swing with an open club face at impact to hit the ball from a tight lie. Your backswing should be straighter back than usual, your arms swinging across your body to finish left of the left shoulder on the follow through. The set up grip change allows the club face to return in an open position; keep the left hand leading.

The correct technique for the fade; the balls indicate the flight path.

THE DRAW

Before taking this shot where the ball flies from right to left, visualize the ball flight you need to avoid any trees or obstacles between you and your target. When you have chosen this path, it will become your target and you can adjust your stance and body alignment accordingly.

QUICK TIP: Be realistic

Only attempt those shots about which you feel confident and know you are capable of hitting well. Do not be unrealistic out on the course. The best place to cultivate the more difficult shots in the game of golf is the practice ground.

The correct set up for the draw with the ball positioned towards the back of the stance.

Club selection and set up

To create anti-clockwise (right to left) spin on the ball, contact it with a closed club face. This will reduce the loft so you should select a more lofted club than for a fade. Try using your 6 or 7 iron for this shot. Use a strong grip, both hands clockwise on the club (thumbs right of the centre line). As you look down, you will see more of the back of your left hand and less of the back of your right than normal. The club face should be closed with the ball positioned towards the back of the stance. Your feet and body should aim to the right. The ball will land with overspin causing more run, so allow for this.

The balls on the ground show the right-to-left flight path of the ball.

The swing

For this shot, make your backswing more rounded, so it travels on an inside curve. Your forearms and hands should rotate through impact and you should follow through towards your initial target point. Don't rush; keep the swing smooth, rhythmic and unhurried on an in-to-out path. To get a draw, the club face should be slightly closed at impact.

Through impact, the club face should be slightly closed; the forearms and hands rotate.

QUICK TIP: Perfecting the draw

- Your feet and body should aim to the right.
- The club face should be toed in slightly (closed).
- Your hands should be further right on the grip.
- The ball should be towards middle of the stance.
- The backswing should be more rounded.
- Rotate forearms and hands through impact.
- Follow through towards the initial aim point.

PLAYING HIGH SHOTS

A high shot is useful when you need to clear obstacles such as trees, so use a sufficiently lofted club. Your aim is to get the ball back in play so don't take risks; you may well end up in an even worse position.

The set up and swing

You need a good lie for this shot. Set up with the ball further forward than normal in your stance, more towards your left foot. Your hands should be level or just behind the ball with the weight more on the right side. Your right shoulder should be lower than the left shoulder with your head behind the ball. Swing your arms higher in the backswing, and when you swing through impact your weight should be more on the right side than normal.

Set up with the ball further forward in your stance, more towards the left foot.

QUICK TIP: Key points for a high shot

- The ball should be further forward in your stance.
- Your hands should be level with the ball.
- Your weight should favour the right leg.
- Keep your head still until after impact.
- Take a divot, and get to the bottom of the ball.

On the backswing use more wrist action. At impact, you will feel the right hand working under the left. Make sure you keep your head still and behind the ball until after impact.

PLAYING LOW SHOTS

Sometimes you may want to produce a low ball flight, and a 5 or 6 iron is perfect for this, provided that you reduce the loft by keeping your hands forward of the club head through impact.

The set up and swing

When setting up for a low shot, the ball should be positioned towards the back of the stance with the hands well forward and your weight favouring the left side. The toe of the club face should be turned in. Choke down on the grip a little and make a wide swing to punch the ball forwards. The ball will travel a long way so a half- to three-quarters swing will be adequate. You should follow through with your hands, arms and club pointing at the target.

Set up with the ball well back in your stance and the club face toed in slightly.

QUICK TIP: Key points for a low shot

When you are confronted with a situation that necessitates hitting a low shot, follow the guidelines below:

● The ball should be towards your right foot.
● Your hands should be forward of the ball, and level with the middle of your left thigh.
● You should choke down on the grip a little.
● The club face should be toed in slightly.
● Your weight should favour the left leg.
● You need to make a wide swing.

When playing a low shot, choke down on the grip a little and make a wide, firm-wristed swing to punch the ball forwards and finish pointing towards the target.

BALL ABOVE FEET

This shot has a tendency to fly right to left in a draw or hook shape. To execute this shot successfully, your posture in the set up should be straighter, with less bend from the waist. Do not push back on your heels too much. Move your hands lower down the club grip, making the playing length of your club shorter (choking down on the club), and always aim a little right of your target. The ball should always be positioned towards the centre of your stance.

Position the ball in the centre of your stance and to the right, as shown by the clubs on the ground.

QUICK TIP: Setting up for different lies

Out on the fairway, you will encounter a number of different lies: sloping, uphill and downhill. In order to make successful shots from slopes and trouble spots, you will need to make several changes to your set up and have a sound technique.

At address, do not bend your hips and knees too much. This will cause your hands to be too low and you will end up hitting a bad shot.

The swing

To make good contact with a ball that is above your feet, you must make a flatter, more rounded swing than usual on the backswing and follow through. This will have the effect of producing a right-to-left shot in a draw or hook shape. The ball will travel approximately the same distance as usual, even though the slope has brought it nearer to you.

QUICK TIP: Fairway woods

If the lie is not too severe and you need distance, you could play a fairway wood instead of an iron.

Choking down on the club

Due to a combination of swing path and face angle, this shot has a tendency to fly from right to left, and the slope will bring it slightly closer to you at address. Allow for this by moving your hands a little down the grip of the club, making the playing length of the club shorter. This is commonly known as 'choking down on the club'.

With the ball above the feet, your posture should be straighter and the swing plane flatter. A more rounded swing produces a shot that flies in the desired direction from right to left.

BALL BELOW YOUR FEET

Many golfers detest this shot, but if you make the right adjustments to your set up and keep your balance it is not difficult. Take a practice swing before hitting your shot. It is an effective way of testing out your balance.

The set up

This is an awkward stance with the ball lower than normal, so stand a little closer than usual, positioning the ball forward in your stance towards your left foot. Bend more from your hips than your knees; increase your knee flex to maintain your balance and help you to get down to the ball. Aim to the left of your target and use a longer club than normal, holding it at full length and gripping it at the end. Your hands should be a little in front of the ball at address. More of your weight will be towards your toes, so you should retain enough over your heels to keep your balance. Try not to feel as though you are going to topple forwards towards the ball.

At address, bend more from your hips and aim to the left. Flex your knees to maintain your balance.

QUICK TIP: Keep your balance

For this shot, you must bend forwards from your hips, using your knees to maintain your balance. You may find this difficult as it is easy to lose your balance and fall forwards towards the ball. Practise this often, swinging smoothly, and you will soon master the delicate balancing position and hit good shots.

The swing

Your swing plane will be more upright and you must retain the spine angle to stay low through impact. Adopting the correct posture will make a more balanced follow through possible. The ball flight will tend to go from left to right, which will cause the ball to fade and lose distance, so you should use a less lofted club than normal. Do not try to hit the ball too hard when you are executing this shot; you should feel as though you are punching it away with your hands and arms.

Keep your balance for this shot and be careful to avoid overswinging.

For the ball below feet shot, you should bend more from your hips and aim to the left. Your backswing should be more upright with a low spine angle through impact with the ball to create a balanced follow through.

UPHILL LIES

This is a lie where the ball is positioned on an upslope, sloping towards the target. It is a relatively easy shot to play because the uphill slope doubles as your very own launching pad to get the ball airborne.

The set up and swing

Your body weight should be parallel with the slope, favouring the right leg (lower foot). Use a less lofted club and aim slightly right of your intended target. Position the ball forwards in your stance towards your left foot (the higher one). Your swing angle into the ball must correspond with the slope, so your follow through must rise more quickly so as not to bury the club into the ground.

Note how the body weight corresponds with the slope, favouring the right leg.

When you swing, allow for the change in ball flight by aiming slightly right of your intended target. Move the ball forwards in your stance and shift more of your body weight to your lower foot before taking your normal swing.

QUICK TIP: Steep uphill and downhill lies

In these situations where the slope is very severe, your balance can be precarious. Your best bet is to play the ball back to a flat piece of ground and start again. Use only a small swing with a more lofted club, but keep your aim and ball position the same as for playing from normal uphill and downhill lies.

The slope and your body weight staying back on your right side will cause the ball to fly much higher than usual, and you will tend to pull it to the left, hence your aim adjustment.

Adapt your technique

It is important throughout this shot to focus on maintaining good balance and rhythm and to play within your capabilities – do not attempt to emulate your golfing heroes on the Tour and try to pull off a miracle shot. Just adapt your usual technique, as described above, in order to accommodate the slope.

DOWNHILL LIES

This is exactly the opposite of an uphill lie; it is a lie where the ball is on a downslope, sloping down towards the target. Because the slope is pointing downwards, it is more difficult to get the ball airborne.

Set up

When you are playing this shot, you must not try to lift the ball, so take care that you choose a 5 iron or a more lofted club, which will become less lofted as a result of the way in which the slope influences how you stand. When setting up for this shot, it is also extremely important that you allow for the flight of the ball, and you accommodate the slope with your body parallel to it.

An incorrect set up from a downslope, leaning back into the slope with the ball too far forwards.

QUICK TIP: Allowing for the slope

Keep your body weight parallel to the slope with your spine at right angles to it, favouring the left leg – don't lean back. Your right shoulder should be higher than the left. Always aim slightly left of target as the ball will curve to the right in flight. Position the ball towards the centre of your stance, towards your higher foot.

On your backswing, the club head should go back more quickly than usual, following the line of the slope.

The swing

You will find that your club head should start to rise more quickly than usual on the backswing, and then it should follow the line of the slope on returning to the ball. As the club head descends to the ball and through impact (see the photographic sequence below), it should follow the line of the slope. You must stay lower after the ball to correspond with the slope. The shot will fly lower, and there will be a tendency for the ball to fade from left to right.

QUICK TIP: Club selection

Do not attempt to hit the ball with a straight-faced club off a downslope. A 5 iron is the longest club that you should contemplate using, unless you are very proficient at this shot.

Set up with your body weight corresponding with the slope and favouring the left leg. Maintaining your rhythm and balance is the key to success with this tricky shot. Make sure you use a lofted club to get the ball airborne.

PUTTING

The average round of golf is composed of 37 per cent long game and 63 per cent short game, so you can see how good putting can lower your scores. The skills needed are touch and feel, making it possible for the slightest woman to compete on equal terms with even the strongest man. Practising your putting regularly will help improve your game rapidly.

> **QUICK TIP: Getting ahead**
> Good putting can ease the pressure on your chipping and pitching and lead to more relaxed and successful play.

THE PUTTING GRIP

Good preparation is the key to successful golf, and putting is no exception to this rule. You need to perfect an effective and consistent relationship between your hands and the way you place them upon the handle of your putter. Your putting grip will be slightly different from the one you normally use for full shots, and you must decide which one to use.

The overlapping grip

There are several ways of holding a putter. Some golfers favour the overlapping, or Vardon, grip where all the fingers of the left hand are placed around the handle, with the thumb lying on top of the handle and the back of the hand facing the target. The ring finger of the right hand is placed against the index finger of the left hand. The remaining fingers of the right hand are folded round the handle, with the little finger resting in the recess between the index and second fingers of the left hand. The thumb of the right hand is placed upon the top of the handle, which ensures that the palm of the right hand is facing the target. This used to be the most popular grip.

QUICK TIP: Hand size

Golfers with small hands may find that when the little finger of the right hand overlaps the index finger of the left hand, it rests on top of the index finger. However, for people with long fingers, the little finger will rest in the cleft between the index finger and the third finger.

Building the grip

The correct way to build the overlapping grip is to lay the grip of the club across your left hand from a point at the first joint of the index finger through the palm into the butt of the hand. Close your fingers round the club shaft with the thumb pointing down the centre of the shaft. Place the palm of the right hand facing the hole, the little finger of the right hand overlapping the index finger of the left hand. The thumb of the right hand will be pointing down the shaft.

Lay the grip of the putter across your left hand and then close the fingers round the shaft, with the thumb pointing down the centre of the shaft.

Place the palm of the right hand facing the hole, the little finger of the right hand overlapping the index finger of the left hand. The right thumb points down the shaft.

The interlocking grip

In this grip the left hand takes the same position as in the overlapping grip (see page 110), but, as the right hand closes around the handle, the little finger of the right hand interlocks with the index finger of the left hand, thereby interlocking the hands together.

Build the interlocking grip with the shaft resting across your left hand (above). Extend the left index finger and place the palm of the right hand facing the hole.

Instead of overlapping the little finger over the left-hand index finger, interlock it between the index finger and third finger (opposite).

The reverse overlap grip

This grip has now become the most widely used of all the putting grips. What makes it so effective is that it minimizes wrist action by placing the handle more in the palms of both hands. This produces a more passive grip and permits the shoulder to initiate the pendulum action of the putting stroke.

Building the grip

To build the reverse overlap grip, start by placing the club handle diagonally across the heel pad of your left hand. Only the tips of the fingers should be on

the grip; your left index finger will not be on the club. It is extended downwards and lying on the fingers of the right hand with your left thumb placed on the top of the handle running straight down. The handle rests at the base of the index finger of the right hand, with your right ring finger lying against the middle finger of your left hand.

The reverse overlap grip.

The handle will run diagonally up across the palm towards a spot just under the heel pad. The club should not rest in your right palm. The fleshy part of your hand, just under the heel pad, should rest against the middle finger of your left hand. Your right thumb should be just to the left of the handle, so it won't exert pressure and influence the putting stroke. The right hand will be turned slightly clockwise or under just a few degrees to maintain a relaxed position.

Start building the grip with your left-hand index finger extended. The right-hand grip should also be as before but without any overlapping or interlocking. All the fingers of the right hand take up their natural position on the grip, but the index finger of the left hand will overlap the first three fingers of the right hand.

THE PUTTING STROKE

An efficient putting stroke will roll the ball across the green on the correct line and at the right speed for any distance. You must keep the ball rolling on the putting surface, not jumping up into the air or it is more likely to pull up short of the hole.

Pendulum putting

For a consistent feel for distance and line, contact the ball with the sole of the putter horizontal (parallel) to the ground. Avoid hitting the ball on a downward or upward approach, which will cause it to hop.

Most good golfers use the pendulum putting stroke as it is easier to obtain level contact. The putter is kept level with the ball's equator for at least 23cm (9in) on either side of the ball, which is positioned just inside the left heel. The backswing and the forward swing are equal in length.

The distance that the ball travels will be governed by the length of your stroke.

For the pendulum stroke, the putter should meet the ball with its sole parallel to the ground (top left and right). Don't hit it too much on the upswing (below left) with the hands too far behind the putter head. Nor should you hit down on the ball too much (below right) with your hands too far in front of the putter face.

QUICK TIP: Avoiding excessive wrist break

This method is designed to minimize hand and wrist action with no breaking or hinging of the left wrist on the forward swing. Excessive wrist break and over-active hands may cause inconsistent ball contact and poor control of distance. This stroke promotes the feeling of a stroke, not a hit.

The set up

Stand comfortably over the ball, holding the putter lightly. Try to relax, focusing on the line you want the ball to take. Bend forwards more from your hips than for your set up for other shots. If you were to drop a vertical line down from the front of your shoulders, it should fall a few inches in front of your toe line. Don't put all your weight on your toes; it should be distributed evenly between the balls of your feet and your heels. You do not have to keep your arms straight; each elbow can point inwards towards the corresponding hip bone.

A normal golf shot set up (left). See how the grip on the club handle is different from the putting one (right) and the arms are straighter and not so close to the body.

QUICK TIP: Shaft and grip

The putter shaft is much closer to a vertical line than it is for a normal golf shot and you will be standing much closer to the ball than usual. You will also find that the putter grip falls more into the palm of your left hand than for full shots.

Do not press your arms hard against your body or you won't be able to keep it still while your arms move. Try to hold your hands high, giving the wrists a better chance to remain firm throughout your stroke.

A good putting set up (left), with the eyes over the ball, hands away from the legs, and elbows pointing inwards towards the hips. The set up (right) shows the distance you would stand from the ball if hitting a full shot with an iron or similar club.

The grip and putter shaft

As we have seen, several putting grips can be used successfully for putting, but the reverse overlap grip (see page 116) is most common and has the best chance of success. The length of the putter that you use is an important consideration. If the shaft is too long, it will cause you to stand up too straight with your arms too bent. If it is too short, you will crouch over too much and your arms will be too straight.

Too long a putter shaft (above) will make your posture too upright and the eye line will not be over the ball; a short putter shaft will produce a crouched posture.

Your hands should be held high (right) for the pendulum stroke. If they are too close to the body (far right), this will produce a wristy action.

QUICK TIP: Body alignment

For a normal straight putt, your feet and shoulder alignment should be parallel with the ball-to-hole line. Visualize a rectangle where the point at which your feet are aimed is equidistant from the hole, as your feet are from the ball.

Your feet, knees, hips and shoulders should all point parallel to your target line. The ball to the right of the hole is the same distance from the hole as the player stands from the object ball.

Ball position

You can experiment with positioning the ball in some different places in your stance but, ideally, it should be just inside the left heel and no further back than the centre. You want to contact the ball on a level approach, neither upwards nor downwards. Unlike other golf shots, your eye line should be directly over the ball. The easiest method of checking this is to get

Hold a ball in your right hand on the bridge of your nose (left) and then simply drop it (right). It should hit the ball on the ground if your eye line is over the ball.

into your set-up position and then take a second ball and hold it between your eyes, on the bridge of your nose. Let it fall and you will find that it should land on top of the ball you are playing.

This set up shows the correct position for the ball just inside the left heel.

QUICK TIP:
The sweet spot

Position the ball in line with the sweet spot on the putter blade or you will get a mishit and the ball will miss its target. You can find the sweet spot by holding the putter up in the air with two fingers at the grip end while tapping the putter face with your forefinger. When you tap the face and it swings without deviating or twisting, you have found the sweet spot where you must strike the ball.

The pendulum stroke

To produce the correct pendulum movement, you need to form a triangle of your arms and shoulders and which moves from a fulcrum at the back and base of your neck. Focus on keeping your legs, body and head very steady and feel your shoulders rocking back and forth.

Performing the pendulum stroke

This movement is not the same as the full golf swing in which the shoulders turn around the trunk of the body. During the backswing, your right shoulder should move up slightly as your left shoulder moves down. On the follow through, the reverse happens – the left shoulder moves up and the right moves down.

QUICK TIP: Pre-stroke drills

Do not stand absolutely motionless for too long before you putt. To prevent yourself freezing over the ball, you should try the following drills:

● Tap the ground lightly just behind the ball before you start your stroke.

● Do not push down into the ground by resting your weight on the putter.

● Make some small movements with your feet to get really settled before you take your stroke.

● Press your hands forward towards the target, just prior to the take away.

QUICK TIP: Body weight

Your weight should be distributed slightly in favour of your
left leg, approximately 60:40. As in all golf shots, the set up
is of paramount importance when putting, and you cannot
putt well from a bad address position.

It is essential that the putter grip, shaft and head move
at the same pace and at a constant speed throughout.
The length of your putting stroke will govern the
distance that the ball will travel after impact.

You may swivel your
head to have a final
check along the
putter line, but do
not lift it up or down,
and make sure you
keep your body still.

The putting stroke as seen sideways on: note how the left shoulder has moved down, right shoulder up from the set up. The putter grip, shaft and head move at the same pace.

Viewed from the front, notice how the impact position is identical to address. The triangle and putter shaft relationship is maintained throughout the putting stroke.

JUDGING DISTANCE

Misjudging speed, especially on middle- and long-range putts, can lead to poor results and misjudged distance. How often have you been six feet short or six feet long on a putt? Even on a very badly directed line, you are unlikely to be more than two or three feet off line.

Developing a feel for distance

The pendulum putting stroke is generally more reliable in promoting a better feel for distance than a hitting action. The backswing and follow through correspond in length, like the movement of a clock pendulum. Always ensure that the backswing is sufficiently long to

permit gradual acceleration without having to speed it up with your hands. Try to think of the ball as if it just happens to be in the way of the putter head as it moves smoothly through the middle part of the stroke rather than hitting at it consciously.

Longer putts require a longer backswing and through swing – you do not have to hit the ball harder.

Distance swing drill

Practise your putting stroke without aiming at a target. Take six balls on to the putting green and then make pendulum strokes of varying lengths:

- Two balls with a 15-cm (6-in) backswing and through swing.
- Two balls with a 30-cm (12-in) swing.
- Two balls with a 45-cm (18-in) movement, and so on.

Keep the pace of your stroke constant, focusing on making a consistent strike, and notice how the roll distance varies according to the stroke length. Place a tee in the ground 30cm (12in) behind the ball and another tee 30cm (12in) after the ball. Position it about an inch outside your intended target line.

QUICK TIP: Length

This easy putting exercise will provide you with a simple visual guide to the length of your stroke on either side of the ball.

Place a tee 30cm (12in) on either side of the ball to help develop a backswing and a follow through which are of equal length.

DIRECTION

The ball's direction is influenced by your aim, the face of your putter at impact, and the swing line that the putter head moves along on either side of the ball. The arc followed by the head is less pronounced than for a full swing. On short putts, there should be no curve in the swing and the putter should move on a straight line through the ball. However, on longer putts, the swing will curve slightly inside on the backswing and follow through.

Put into practice the distance swing drill by putting from three different distances. You can judge the overall distance of a long putt more easily if you get into the good habit of breaking the putt down into several smaller distances.

The channel created by the tees on the ground shows how the putter head swing should remain parallel to the target line.

QUICK TIP: Distance and direction

Always remember the following points when putting:

● The putter face must aim at your target – the hole – for a straight putt.

● Your feet and body line should aim slightly left.

● Your shoulders, arms, hands and putter shaft should all move together in unison as one unit.

● Your legs, body and head should stay still throughout.

● The backswing and forward swing should always be of equal length.

● The pace of the pendulum putting stroke should stay constant throughout.

HOW TO READ BREAK

You will learn how to visualize a straight line to the hole, but reading break is more difficult. There are so many factors that can affect the way in which a ball reacts to the contours on a green. To read break successfully, you must evaluate the green conditions and determine the strength and speed of stroke you need to achieve the curvature to the hole.

Calculate the break

Crouch down behind the ball. Try and visualize how it will curve and break. Get a mental picture of the ball rolling on a straight line towards the hole. This will help you to calculate at what point, and by how much, it will break from this line.

The grain of the grass

The grain will affect the speed and break of a putt, especially where a coarse grass is sown, usually in hot climates. If you are putting down-grain, where the blades of grass lean towards the hole, the ball will tend to run faster; if the grain is towards you, the speed of the ball will be slower.

On a straight putt, where the grain runs across the line, you may need to aim outside the hole. Where the grain runs in the opposite direction, on a left-to-right or right-to-left break, you must decide how it could affect

QUICK TIP: Practice drill

Choose a six-foot putt on a sloping section of a putting green, then place four balls around the hole in positions with a different break. Get down 10 feet behind the ball with your eye-line as low as possible. Visualize a straight line to the hole and then try to work out the amount of borrow needed.

the break and then judge the margin you borrow. Straight putts with the grain tend to be very fast but putts against the grain are much slower. A good tip is that if the grass is shiny and lying flat and away from you, there is a down grain. Conversely, if the grass is dull and against you, there is an up grain.

The three tee pegs on the left indicate the slope and the break. In between the second and third tee pegs is the point of break.

CHIPPING & PITCHING

An effective short game can make all the difference between winning or losing a match. Although not as glamorous as the long game, it is well worth perfecting it if you want to lower your handicap. Don't waste your practice sessions just thrashing away with your driver; concentrate on your wedge and putter and watch those scores come tumbling down.

CHIPPING

One of the simplest yet most important shots in golf is the chip from the fringe of the green. Many golfers make it look complicated, but, played correctly, it really is simple and can help to lower your scores.

The set up

You use the same technique, whichever club you use (your wedge or 7 iron), except that for the same length of shot the more lofted wedge needs to be struck more firmly because of the greater backspin it creates. In the address position, open your stance a little but no more than feels comfortable and natural. This will enable you to judge the line and length more accurately than from a squarer position. Place the ball back in your stance nearer the right foot. Hold the club towards the bottom of the grip (an inch or two nearer the shaft) for extra

The set up for a simple running chip with a 7 iron. Note the comfortable, open stance which makes it easy to judge both the distance and direction.

To play a good chip shot, judge how the ball will react on landing. Keep your left wrist firm through the hitting area with the club face facing your intended target.

control, and stand close to the ball with your arms close to your body. Shift most of your weight on to your left foot and place your hands well in front of the club head so that the shaft slopes towards the target.

QUICK TIP: The right club

Play the chip with a pitching wedge or 7 iron. With practice, you will soon be able to judge the amount of carry and run.

Playing the shot

To play the chip shot successfully, keep the club head low to the ground throughout the swing, allowing the wrists to break only slightly in the backswing with your weight remaining on the left side. Make a smooth, unhurried brushing stroke through the ball with the hands leading all the way.

QUICK TIP: Hands

Allow the loft on the club face to lift the ball slightly. If you make the backswing purely with your hands, the right hand will try to scoop the ball up on the upswing and this will result in a poor shot.

Notice how the hands lead the club face through impact and all the way through to the completion of the swing; there's no flicking of the wrists.

QUICK TIP: Chipping from the rough

A chip shot from the rough by the side of the green will run further than one played from shorter grass on the apron of the green. The longer grass between the club head and ball will reduce the backspin. When you set up for this shot, position the ball more towards the right foot and open the club face a fraction. Use a wedge for this shot and accelerate through the ball with an outside-to-in swing line. The wrists should cock earlier on the backswing in order to create a steeper takeaway and a sharper descending arc into the ball.

This shot is not unlike a long putt with a more lofted club in which you allow the loft on the club face to carry the ball through the air for the short distance.

Avoiding common faults

Try to avoid the most common faults which are:
- A bad set up with the ball too far forward and the hands and weight too far back.
- 'Scooping' the ball into the air using too much wrist action.
- Leaning back on the right foot.

If you tend to hit poor chip shots, one of these faults may be causing the problem. So try to analyze where you are going wrong and which of the above applies to you. Practise your chipping and you will soon be able to roll three shots into two around the greens on a regular basis. Keep it simple and it will help you to reduce your handicap.

PITCHING

The short, fairly high pitch looks so easy when the pros put the ball next to the flag, yet many beginners have problems with this shot. The swing is just the full swing in miniature, but judging distance accurately is vital.

The set up

Many people who can play a full shot and cope with a simple chip from just off the edge of the green regard the pitch as a 'clever half shot' which is best left to the experts. However, the pitch is, after a putt, the most commonly played shot in golf and is worth mastering if you want to reduce your handicap. For a pitch shot, make some minor modifications to your normal set up. Position the ball in the centre of your stance with your hands ahead of the ball. Your weight should be a little more on the left side than usual. Addressing the ball in this way will help produce a sharper downswing into the ball and impart more backspin.

QUICK TIP: Don't fluff!

Many beginners playing a pitch shot make the common mistake of leaning back on to the right foot in an attempt to scoop the ball high into the air, but this will usually result in a fluffed or thinned shot. Try to trust your swing and allow the loft on your club to do the work and create the shot for which it was designed.

The swing

You need the same swing as for a full wedge shot but, as you are not hitting the the ball so far, less of it. If a full wedge flies 90 yards, aim to take half as much swing for a 45-yard pitch. Strike the ball with a smoothly accelerating club head. Think of the relationship between length of swing and length of shot in terms of a clock face. If your backswing reaches 10 o'clock, your follow through will finish at 2 o'clock. If your backswing goes to 8 o'clock, the follow through should stop at 4 o'clock. Your stance will become narrower and progressively more open for shorter shots. Strike the ball positively and slightly on the downswing, so the grooves on the club face bite

When pitching, the same principles apply as for any golf shot. On this shot of 60 yards, your hands will reach 10 o'clock on the backswing and will swing through to finish at about 2 o'clock.

into its surface and produce backspin. The loft on your club will lift the ball into the air, so keep your club face square through impact and into the follow through to create maximum backspin.

Practise your pitching

The pitch is a useful shot when you need more height on the ball, e.g. lofting the ball over a greenside bunker. Practise hitting different lengths of bunker shot, without varying the distance you hit behind the ball. Just adjust the length of your swing, as you would for a pitch from grass. Don't try to scoop the ball out of a bunker, even if it is close to the lip and needs to rise steeply. You need to make your stance a little more open with the ball positioned further forward, and then you can make the ball rise almost vertically.

This shot travelled 35 yards. The hands swung back to 8 o'clock on the backswing and round to 4 o'clock at the finish.

QUICK TIP: A ball in its own pitch mark

If the ball is deeply embedded in its own pitch mark in the sand, you must change your technique.

1 Place the ball opposite the right foot. Use a steep backswing, straight back from the ball in line with the target.

2 Hit firmly down into the sand 7–10cm (3–4in) behind the ball; do not try to follow through. It will blast out lower than normal, with very little backspin, and run a long way.

PITCHING OUT OF A BUNKER

For a standard bunker shot, always use a sand iron, which is designed specifically for this job, and don't try to pull off any miracles – just play within your limitations. If the shot seems too difficult to attempt, do not automatically aim for the flag. Just take a penalty drop into an easier position within the bunker and then get out on to the green. It's not worth dropping more shots by trying to pull off heroic recoveries. Nor should you try to lift the ball cleanly off the sand – this is one of the most difficult shots in the game.

QUICK TIP: Overcome your fear

If you are unlucky and your ball lands in a bunker, don't panic and don't attempt to lean backwards and lift the ball up and out. Just practise the method described and you will overcome your fear and become a proficient and confident bunker player.

This is the swing you should use for all but the most unusual shots from bunkers. It should be smooth, unhurried and rhythmic. Do not be tempted to force your swing but focus instead on swinging the club head down into the sand and through to the target without rushing.

PITCHING OVER BUNKERS

This shot often strikes fear into the average golfer, who instinctively feels the need to hit the ball with a high, gentle flight in order to stop it quickly. However, most bunkers do not have a high lip and all you need to do is carry the ball past them. Ignore the sand and pick out a spot on the green as your landing area. Using your most lofted club, swing at the ball smoothly and strike it crisply forward and down. Keep the weight more on the left side to encourage the contact you are seeking.

Play the shot like a normal pitch but with maximum backswing to get the ball as close as possible to the pin.

QUICK TIP: Don't lift

You must not try to lift a ball over a bunker; just swing firmly and smoothly down and through the ball. Your sand wedge has a loft of between 52 and 60 degrees – that's more than enough to generate both the height and backspin you need.

You are looking for backspin, not height, so trust your swing and the loft on your club to produce the shot you want. Never try to lift the ball into the air, which is a recipe for disaster. This stroke requires the maximum amount of backswing in order to hit the ball near to the pin. Use a sand iron to make use of its great loft and play the shot like any other pitch.

CURING SWING FAULTS

Most golfers encounter some problems in their game at one time or another, but these can all be remedied. Understanding what causes these faults helps you to avoid their consequences and learn how to cure them. Overcome the most dreaded bad shots and you'll soon be hitting the ball again with confidence and precision.

THE SLICE

This is a weak shot which lacks power and often will fly higher than it should do. It always curves to the right because the golfer strikes the ball with the club face open, thereby aiming off to the left.

The cause

This shot pattern is usually due to an incorrect grip and hand action, which cause the club face to return to the ball in an open position, aiming to the right of the ball-to-target line, making the ball finish right of target.

QUICK TIP: Slice checklist
- The lie of the club may be too flat.
- The grip may be too thick.
- The club shaft may be too stiff.
- Keep the club face square at address.

These hands are in a weak position as they are turned too far to the left. Correct your grip by moving both hands to the right, so the 'V's are pointing more towards your right shoulder than your chin. Do not grip the handle too tightly.

A vicious circle

Most people's natural reaction to slicing is to start aiming even further left to compensate for it. However, the more you allow for your slice, the more likely you are to perpetuate it. It is a vicious circle because by aiming considerably left, your swing path is likely to go the same way and you must deliver the club face in an open position, or the ball will fly straight left.

The remedy

When you set up, your left hand should hold the grip in the fingers, but not too tightly. The 'V's between the thumb and first finger of both hands should point towards your right shoulder, not your chin. Your feet and shoulders should be parallel to the target line, and your left shoulder should be higher than the right one. You must not position the ball too far forward in your stance as this will contribute to an open club face; it should be further back towards the right foot.

The swing

Beware of rolling your hands and opening the club face on the takeaway; make a more rounded, flatter swing. At the top of the backswing, the club face should be on the same angle as the shoulder plane. Make sure that you make a full shoulder turn, with your weight on the right leg.

The downswing to follow through

On the downswing, you must swing the club down from the top with your hands and arms from the inside, moving your arms in unison close to your right hip. On the throughswing, you should move your arms away from the left hip to clear the left side. The back of your left hand and forearm should rotate within the arc of the swing, and the club shaft must point downwards on the follow through as your weight shifts onto your firm left leg.

THE HOOK

Unlike the slice, which tends to afflict beginners and poor players, the hook is associated with good golfers and can be devastating, especially if it causes the ball to land in hazards and trouble spots around the course.

The cause

A hooked ball begins its flight to the right of the intended target line, then curves severely to the left. It tends to fly lower and land with topspin, making it a particularly destructive shot because it runs further off-line. Hooked shots are hit with the club face closed at impact, which causes them to bend to the left when airborne.

Too strong a grip

Hooking is often associated with a strong grip: holding the club with the left hand too far on top of the grip and the right hand too far under. This results in the club face returning to the ball in a closed position (aiming left of the target), creating a swing plane that is too flat on the backswing and too upright on the follow through.

QUICK TIP: Hook checklist

- The lie of your club may be too upright.
- The grip may be too thin.
- The club shaft may be too flexible.
- Your ball may be too far back in your stance.

The grip is too strong and the hands turned too far to the right. The left hand is too far on top of the grip and the right hand is too far underneath it. If both 'V's point near to or outside the right shoulder, move them to the left. When you look down at your left hand, you should see only two knuckles.

Because most right-handed golfers are considerably stronger in their right hand, it tends to take over, so the left hand and wrist collapse. When things go wrong in golf, our natural reaction to try and put things rights often has the opposite effect and just makes them worse. In this case, most golfers aim too far right in their set up to compensate. A strong grip will cause the face of the club at the top of the backswing to be pointing skywards in a closed position. This will be reflected at impact when the bottom of the swing arc arrives too early behind the ball and, combined with the swing path going right of target, imparts anti-clockwise spin on the ball, causing it to hook.

The remedy

At address, weaken your grip; position the ball forward in your stance to eliminate a flat swing plane and align your shoulders more to the left. The back of your left hand should face the target. Your right hand should hold more in the fingers (palm facing the target) with light pressure. Grip the club with your hands turned more to the left, the 'V's pointing at your chin. Your feet, knees, hips and shoulders all aim slightly left of target.

The swing

Make your swing path straighter on the backswing. At the top, both wrists should be under the shaft with the toe of the club face pointing downwards. On the downswing, your hips and body should turn to face left of target; as you swing down you must clear the left side. Your hands should swing left of your left shoulder at the finish. Keep your left hand and wrist firm through impact, with the back of your left hand facing the target. The right hand must not overtake and cross over the left too soon.

THE PULL

A pulled shot will fly in a straight line to the left of your intended target. The club face is square relative to the swing path, and thus you do not impart any sidespin on the ball, causing an outside-to-in swing path.

The cause

The pull is related to the slice as the swing path is the same. Some golfers slice with their long straighter-faced clubs and pull the shorter ones. This is because the lofted clubs impart backspin which reduces the amount of sidespin which is associated with the longer clubs.

The remedy

Stop swinging the club head across the line of the ball's intended flight. Check your aim at address: your feet, shoulders and club face may aim to the left. The ball must not be too far forward in your stance and should be inside the left heel.

QUICK TIP: Pull checklist

● On the backswing, make sure that your left shoulder, arms and club head all start moving as one.

● At the top of your backswing, the shaft of the club should be parallel to the target line.

● Keep the club head moving inside the intended line of flight on the downswing.

The club lying on the grass behind the ball shows the correct target line. The club to the left of the ball shows the swing path of the pull with the ball finishing left of the target.

The swing

The backswing should be on a more rounded, flatter plane with a full shoulder turn. Your shoulders, arms, hands and club head should all move together around a fixed axis, so the club head starts moving inside the intended line of ball flight. At the top of the backswing, the club shaft should be parallel to the intended target line. On the downswing, return on the same path, with your arms close to the right hip; transfer your weight from your right side to the left. At impact, the club should reach maximum speed and swing towards the target. On the throughswing, the arms should move away from the left hip. Adopt a higher finishing position.

THE PUSH

This usually occurs when you move your body ahead of the ball before impact, causing it to fly in a straight line to the right of the target. This should not be confused with a slice although the ball finishes in a similar place. The push shot does not curve in flight; it starts to the right of your target and continues to the right.

The cause

This shot belongs to the same family as the hook but the club face is square relative to the swing path instead of closed. If you do this, you don't impart spin on the ball, which flies straight in the direction of the swing path. The push is usually due to one of two faults: swaying to the left on the downswing, so your body and hands are in front of the club head when it hits the ball, or placing the ball too far back in the stance towards the right foot.

The remedy

Check your set up: your feet, shoulders and club face may aim to the right. Check the ball is not too far back in your stance or too far right of centre. Check your grip is not too weak with either or both hands too far round to the left which will cause the club face to open.

The swing

On the backswing, make your swing path straighter to achieve a more upright position. Do not sway; swing

The club on the grass behind the ball indicates the correct target line. The club to the left of the ball shows the swing path of the push with the ball finishing right of your intended target.

the club head on an inclined plane, starting on an inside path close to the grass with the club face facing the ball for a more upright backswing and more effective downswing. The follow through should be more rounded with the hips turned and your stomach facing the target or slightly to the left of it. Do not arch your back too much on the follow through. Your hands should swing to the left of your left shoulder at the finish.

QUICK TIP: Check your swing

If your set up is good and you still hit a push shot, check your swing. It may be you are swinging on an in-to-out path with the club face square to that line.

TOPPING

This swing fault affects some beginners, who will often hit the ball straight along the ground. You may well be afflicted by this shot if you attempt to lift the ball in a scooping action to help get it airborne.

The cause

It occurs when the ball is struck above its equator by an ascending club head, producing a very low shot. Loft is built into a club head and you don't need to compensate for lack of loft and have to 'lift' the ball into the air.

The remedy

For iron shots, especially mid to short irons, strike the ball on the downswing with the club head descending, taking a divot after the ball. Touch the turf at least with the sole of the club to contact the ball squarely in the middle of the club face.

The swing

Your backswing should be more upright. Check that it has not become too flat with you swinging your arms around your body on too rounded an arc. To swing downwards on to the ball, the club head must swing on a straighter line back and up on the backswing. Pull down with the left arm to start the downswing and ensure the wrists uncock fully so the club head gets back to the bottom of the ball. Transfer your weight from your right side to the left on the downswing to strike the ball on a downward path. Your hands should be ahead of the club head at impact.

Instead of the ball being struck on the downswing with the club head descending and taking a divot after the ball, in a topped shot it is hit on the upswing by an ascending club head; no divot is taken.

QUICK TIP: Practice drill

To cure this swing fault, you can practise striking some balls either with a 3 wood or a 6 iron, focusing on making contact with the club head behind the bottom of the ball. At or just before the moment of impact, your left arm and the club shaft should be in a straight line. Check that this is the case.

SKYING

This shot is not really common and it happens only when the ball is teed up using a driver. The flight is extremely high but with little forward momentum, the ball soaring up impressively into the sky but not travelling very far.

The cause

The ball is struck with the top part of the club face, often scratching the head. Most of us have tried to hit the ball further than is humanly possible, leading to a steep backswing and a subsequent chop down into the ball. If the club approaches the ball from too steep an angle on the downswing and the front edge of the sole of the

The moment of impact for a normal swing as opposed to a skied shot (see page 164).

club hits into the ground, the result will be a skied shot. When hitting woods, sweep the club away without hitting the ground, unlike iron shots, which should be struck on the downswing with a divot after the ball. The shaft of a wood is longer and produces a bigger circle with a wider arc for the club head. Thus the sole of the club head can be parallel to the ground at the bottom of the swing arc. If you position the ball forward in your stance (opposite your left instep for a driver) your contact will be at the correct angle to sweep the ball forwards instead of chopping down and producing a skied shot.

The remedy

At address, make sure you position the ball forward in your stance. Some people worry about the height of the tee and believe that teeing the ball high will produce a skied shot but this is not necessarily the case. The important thing is to keep the club head travelling parallel to the ground for several inches before impact. The loft of the club face will lift the ball up into the air; it does not need any help from you. At set up, keep your hands level with the back of the ball with the sole of your club resting flat on the ground.

QUICK TIP: Check your swing

Swinging smoothly, keeping the club head low to the ground at the start of the backswing and parallel to the ground just before impact, can prevent a skied shot.

The swing

At the start of the backswing, keep the club head low to the ground; don't break the wrists too early. Make your swing plane flatter on a more rounded shallow arc. Transfer your weight onto the right side at the top of the backswing with your head behind the ball until after impact. Don't scoop the ball up; you need a low sweep with a slight curve at the beginning of the backswing.

The moment of impact for a skied shot; the downswing is very steep and too much club face is below the centre of the ball at impact. The club chops down on the ball from too steep an angle.

TOEING

This swing fault can happen at any time, and you will know immediately when it does because you will feel the club shaft twisting in your hands at impact.

The cause

Toeing occurs when the toe end of the club strikes the inside half of the ball, causing a shot that flies straight to the right with little power, even though the club face may well be square. A toed shot may appear to be similar to a shank (see page 173).

Get your balance right

To produce this shot, the club head will have been swung on an out-to-in swing path, causing it to return to a point closer to you than it was at address. This is sometimes caused by incorrect balance in the set up. If you stand too close to the ball it will result in too much of your weight being on your heels at address and as you return the ball. Conversely, if you stand too far away from the ball at address, it will make it impossible for your arms to reach the ball.

QUICK TIP: Heels or toes?

To cure this swing fault, you must first try to analyze which of the two scenarios above applies to you, i.e. whether your weight is mainly on your heels or your toes.

Your weight

Ideally, your weight should be distributed evenly between your heels and the balls of your feet, and this is influenced by the distance you stand from the ball. So do not stand in the same way for every shot you take, as this will lead to many poor and erratic hits which are way off target.

Get settled

When addressing the ball, you must move your feet to get settled. Do not just plant them down in a really solid position and then stand absolutely motionless before you take your swing. Instead, have a few waggles with the club head and shuffle your feet slightly to fine tune your balance. Make sure the ball position is correct for your club.

Don't stand too close to the ball; the correct distance from the ball makes you swing on a slightly inclined plane, so the club head moves on an in-to-out swing path. Move your feet a little at address to settle them into the correct position.

The remedy

When you set up, check your balance and distance from the ball. Don't stand too far from it at address as this can cause an out-to-in swing path on a flat plane. You will lose power as you reach out to make contact.

QUICK TIP: Toeing checklist
- At set up, always check your stance and grip.
- Check that the ball position is correct for the club that you are using.
- Check that you are standing the right distance from the ball; not too far away nor too close.
- Think of making a circle as you swing back from the ball at address.
- Check that your left shoulder is under your chin at the top of the backswing.
- Swing the club head smoothly down inside the intended line of flight.
- Don't scoop the ball into the air. Drive down through it.

The swing

For this shot, you want to swing slightly under yourself on an inclined plane. Check that your grip, stance and ball position are correct, and then start making your backswing. The club head should stay close to the ground on a slight curve for about 25cm (10in). At the top of the backswing, your left shoulder should have turned 90 degrees to arrive under your chin.

Swing back down to the ball and through, keeping your left arm extended through impact and also maintaining your spine angle. Swing your arms freely away from your body.

QUICK TIP: Practice drill

A helpful drill for correcting toeing is to substitute two tees for the ball, one of which should be about a ball's width further away from you than the other. Address the closer tee towards the toe of the club and then make a swing that returns to strike both tees. This will encourage contact with the centre of the club face. If you develop this swing fault, this simple practice drill will really help to remedy it.

Practise this simple drill with two tees instead of a ball. Address the closer tee towards the toe of the club and then swing smoothly so the club face strikes both tees centrally at impact.

HITTING BEHIND THE BALL

This fault, which is also referred to as 'hitting fat', is often experienced by golfers. The club head hits the ground behind the ball and the cushion of turf between the club face and ball leads to a severe loss of distance.

The cause

This swing fault can be caused by falling back onto your heels and trying to lift the ball into the air at impact. To prevent this, keep your left side firm at the bottom of your swing. Do not try to 'get under the ball'; allow the loft of the club face to lift it. Visualize your swing arc as a 'U' shape on a slant with the bottom of the 'U' coming after the ball. It is possible that you hit behind the ball because your backswing is too upright and flat. If your divot is very deep and behind the ball, this may well be the case and your backswing is creating a steep angle of attack into the ball.

The remedy

When you set up for your swing, you must make your usual checks at address. Swing back smoothly, gripping the club with about the same pressure in both hands.

QUICK TIP: Depth of divot

The golden rule to bear in mind is: if the divot is deep, swing flatter. If the divot is shallow, swing more upright.

This will help prevent separation between the hands at the top of the backswing which may lead to a 'casting' action on the downswing. Pull down and through towards the target with your left arm, maintaining the left forearm, wrist and back of hand in line through impact. Keep your left leg straight supporting your weight, while your hips rotate to face the target.

Hitting behind the ball can be caused by falling back onto the heels and trying to lift the ball while dipping. Avoid by keeping your left side firm at the bottom of your swing. Keep the left leg straight to support your weight as you rotate towards the target. Do not scoop the ball but keep your left forearm, wrist and back of hand in line.

QUICK TIP: Practice drill

Place a second golf ball approximately 30cm (12in) behind your ball to encourage a downward strike. If you bottom out behind the correct ball, you will contact the wrong one.

THE OVERSWING

This happens when you swing the club back too far and it travels beyond the horizontal at the top of the backswing, so that you are in a position where you lose control. This causes not only loss of length and power but also striking the ground behind the ball.

The cause

A common cause of overswinging is excessive wrist break and letting go of the club or opening up with your left hand at the top of your backswing. To prevent this happening, you should always try to keep your takeaway slow and smooth in order to get into the correct position. Do not lose control by swinging the club back too quickly. In an effort to stop overswinging, you may fail to turn your shoulders and body fully, which will lead to yet more problems and varied, inconsistent shots.

The remedy

Set up for your shot with the left-hand grip held firmly in the base of the fingers (excluding the index finger). Concentrate on using your hands and your wrists earlier in the downswing.

The swing

Swing back slowly, keeping the club head close to the ground in the first part of the takeaway. Your takeaway should not be too steep; keep the club head moving on a shallow arc and break the wrists early to produce a more powerful downswing.

The club shaft has gone below the horizontal position. The left arm has bent too much during the backswing and the swing is now out of control. Keep your left arm as straight as possible.

QUICK TIP: Practice drill

If you have a tendency to overswing, you should try hitting a few balls with a 6 or 7 iron, focusing on keeping your hands and wrists active from the moment you start moving the club back at address. Make sure that you break your wrists early in the takeaway to set yourself up for a more controlled and powerful downswing.

THE SHANK

The most destructive and dreaded shot of all, the shank has shattered the confidence of many golfers. However, it is relatively easy to cure.

The cause

It occurs when the ball is struck from the socket of the club head where the face meets the hosel, causing it to career to the right at a severe angle, usually low. The shank is a difficult fault to analyze as there are three possible causes:

• Returning to the ball with the club face very open.
• Returning to the ball with the club face very closed.
• Returning with the club head to the ball further from you than at address.

Whichever of these faults applies to you, you will probably find that your weight is moving onto your toes with your knees bent. To prevent this happening, you should try to keep your weight towards your heels during the downswing and follow through.

Identifying your fault

If the club face returns in a very open position, the heel and hosel will arrive at the ball first. If the club face is very closed, it will approach on too rounded an arc and can gather the ball into the socket of the club. Consider which ball flight you tend to produce normally.

Shanking may be caused by returning to the ball with the club face very closed (left), or by returning with the club face very open (right). Both will cause the hosel to strike the ball rather than the club face.

The correct position for the club face and ball at address (left); and the position at impact for the shank (right) when the club face returns to the ball and strikes it on the hosel, causing it to fly low and to the right.

If you have a tendency to slice, your shank shot will be of the open face variety; if you tend to hook, however, it will be the closed face version.

QUICK TIP: Occasional shanking

An occasional shank that afflicts a normally straight hitter is likely to be caused by the club head returning further away from you. The divot will be straight and the club face square.

The remedy

The best remedy is to practise the two tees exercise for toeing (see page 168). Place two tees approximately a ball's width apart, one further away from you. Address the furthest one and make a swing that returns to strike only the tee closest to you. Practising on a slope with the ball below your feet may also be helpful if your swing tends to be too flat.

The two tees exercise to cure the shank. Address the tee that is further away from you (left), then swing and strike the tee closer to you (right). Practise regularly and it will help cure this most destructive shot.

GOLF RULES AND ETIQUETTE

We can all benefit from a better understanding of the Rules of golf and how they are applied. This section will give you a basic appreciation of the most commonly used Rules to help you deal with a range of different situations you will encounter out on the course.

ETIQUETTE

Show consideration towards your fellow players. Treat them with respect, be mindful of their safety and take good care of the golf course. How you behave is very important: treat others as you would wish to be treated and leave the course as you would wish to find it.

Replacing divots

If you are hitting a shot from the tee or fairway you may take a divot – a piece of turf dislodged when the club strikes the ground behind the ball. On the fairway, divots must be replaced quickly and trodden down firmly.

QUICK TIP: Raking bunkers

When you leave a bunker, always rake the sand thoroughly to leave it smooth. If there is no rake, use your shoe or the sole of your golf club. Any players coming up behind you should not see any signs that you have been there.

QUICK TIP: Show respect

If a group is behind you waiting to play, don't hold them up by standing around after taking your shots. Move off briskly. Similarly, don't hit your shot while the group in front is still in range. If you use a trolley, park it to the side; don't take it on to the tee or green.

This enables the turf to take root and grow again. If it is left, after 24 hours the grass will die and the course will be scarred. You need not replace a divot on the tee.

Pitch marks

If you play a high approach shot to the green, the impact of the ball may leave an indentation on the putting surface, known as a pitch mark. It is good golf etiquette to repair this immediately with a pitch mark repairer – carry one in your pocket or bag. Just lever the grass around the indentation back into position, then flatten it with the sole of your putter. You can use a tee peg for this if you don't have a repairer.

Be considerate

Always treat your companions with consideration. Don't stand too close when they are taking a practice swing, and stand quietly to the side when they are playing their shots – do not speak or start playing with the coins in your pocket. If you watch the flight of their ball, you can help search for it if it gets lost.

ON THE TEE

The coloured markers on the teeing ground indicate where you should play from. Men usually play off the yellow tees, women off the red, and seniors and juniors off the blue ones. White tees are for competitions. You can tee up anywhere within a rectangle two club lengths back from the markers. You may stand outside the teeing ground to play a ball within it.

Taking a stroke

If you swing the club with the express intention of hitting the ball, the stroke will count, but if you take a practice swing and hit the ground with your club so that the ball falls off the tee, you will not take a penalty. This is because you were not attempting to hit the ball. If the ball falls off the tee before you take a stroke, you will not be penalized because the ball is not in play. However, if it falls off the tee while your club head is descending and you miss it completely, the stroke will count but you will not have to add a penalty.

QUICK TIP: Teeing off

While you are on the tee, make a mental note of the ball you are using: check its make and number. It will be easier to identify if it gets lost or lands in a clump of other balls. Golf etiquette decrees that whoever scores best on the previous hole has 'the honour' of teeing off first on the next one.

OFF THE TEE

When you move away from the tee on to the course, different rules apply if you address the ball and it moves. Even if you're taking a practice swing or have stood over the ball as if to hit it and grounded your club, you will be penalized one stroke. To prevent this happening, never rest your club on the ground behind the ball.

Out of bounds

If you tee up your ball and it goes out of bounds (OB), add a penalty stroke to your score for losing the ball and then tee up another. If, at any time on the course, you hit a ball OB or lose it, you do exactly the same.

The white lines on the ground denote the area that is out of bounds (OB) and within which play is prohibited. It may also be defined by some white stakes.

QUICK TIP: Defining OB

This refers to an area into which you are not allowed to venture and from which play is prohibited. It is defined by white stakes or a line on the ground. If a ball lands OB it is unplayable. However, you may stand out of bounds in order to play a ball that is in bounds.

You must add a penalty stroke and then play your next shot from where you played the previous one; this is known as 'stroke and distance'.

Provisional ball

If you hit a shot that disappears from sight, you can assume that it might be lost and are permitted to hit another ball: a provisional ball. If you can't find the original ball, you may continue play with the provisional one. If this happens, just wait until your companions have played their shots, then tell them that you plan to play a 'provisional ball'; you must use those words and make it clear what you are intending

QUICK TIP: OB boundaries

● Usually OB markers define the boundaries of a golf course but sometimes areas within the course, such as a practice fairway between two holes, can be defined as OB.

● The score card you collect from the pro shop has local rules printed on the back. Check these before you play to find out where the OB boundaries are.

to do. If your first shot travelled, say, 200 yards before going out of sight and the provisional goes only 100 yards, you can hit the provisional as often as needed until it reaches, or goes beyond, the spot where the original is likely to be.

Lost ball

If your ball is lost in the general course of play, you are allowed five minutes in which to look for it. However, if it is lost, you must play 'stroke and distance', i.e. add another stroke to your score and hit the next shot from the same place where you played the last one. If you fail to find a lost ball in a clump of trees or the rough, you are not allowed to drop another ball on the edge of the fairway and take a penalty stroke. Many golfers choose to ignore this Rule because they do not wish to trudge all the way back to the place from which they played their original shot.

QUICK TIP: Searching for a ball

The Rules allow five minutes to search for your ball but sometimes it may be moved in the process of looking for it. This may happen if you, your playing partner or either of your caddies touch or bend the long grass or heather where the ball is nestling; if so, you will incur a penalty stroke and must replace the ball. However, if the ball is moved by your opponent (in matchplay) or anyone on his/her team or by a fellow competitor in strokeplay you do not incur a penalty. In either case, the ball must be replaced.

However, you don't have to do this because you can play with a provisional ball (see page 180), which will now become the ball in play. When you eventually add up your score for the hole, make sure that you count the number of strokes you play with the provisional ball plus the number taken with the original ball, and a penalty stroke.

QUICK TIP: Lost ball exceptions

Note that if a ball is lost in a water hazard, casual water, ground under repair or through damage to the course, different Rules will apply.

Definitions of a lost ball

Declaring that your ball is lost is meaningless unless you can fulfil one of the conditions that are listed below. A ball can only become lost if:

• You cannot find it within five minutes.
• You make a stroke at a provisional ball beyond the point where the original is likely to be.
• You put another ball into play, e.g. not clearly declaring that you are playing a provisional.

Obstructions

In golf, an obstruction is defined as anything artificial, such as benches, the sides of roads and paths, cigarette ends and tin cans. The only exceptions to this rule are objects that define out of bounds, any part of an immovable man-made object that is out of bounds, and any construction declared to be an integral part of the course. If you are not sure, then you should look at the local rules on the back of your scorecard.

Taking relief

You may take relief from an obstruction anywhere on the course with the exception of immovable obstructions in water hazards. If the obstruction is movable, you are permitted to move it without being penalized. If the ball is moved in the process of moving the object, you may replace it. If your ball was on or in the obstruction, after removing the obstruction, you must drop the ball as near as possible to the spot where it lay – the exception to this rule is on the green where you place rather than drop it. However, if the obstruction is not movable, as in the case of a telegraph pole or a pylon, and it interferes with your stance or your intended line of swing, you are allowed to take relief without incurring a penalty.

QUICK TIP: Obstructions

These are artificial, man-made objects. If an immovable object interferes with your stance or intended swing path on the course, you make take relief without penalty within one club length. If the obstruction is movable you may dispose of it without penalty. In contrast, a loose impediment is a natural object that can be moved at any time outside a hazard as long as you do not move the ball as well.

QUICK TIP: The golden rule

The Rules do not distinguish between the fairway, rough, trees and other parts of the golf course. The golden rule is that the 'nearest point of relief' refers to relief from the obstruction – if that happens to be in the middle of a large patch of wiry heather or a gorse bush, then you have to accept it and play accordingly.

How to take relief

Find the nearest point of relief, which is not nearer the hole, avoids interference or requiring you to drop in a hazard or on a putting green, and drop your ball within one club length of that point. If you drop the ball twice and are still not able to take your shot, e.g. when a ball keeps rolling into a bunker, you may place it on the spot where it landed the second time you dropped it.

Dropping the ball

You should stand with your arm straight out at shoulder height and drop the ball within one club length of the nearest point of relief. It may roll up to a further two club lengths away, as long as it goes no nearer to the hole. The only exceptions to this are dropping in an unplayable lie (see below) or from a lateral water hazard, in which case you may drop within two club lengths and the ball may roll up to two club lengths away but no nearer the hole.

If your ball has landed in an unplayable lie, e.g. a gorse bush, declare it unplayable to your playing partners. Measure two club lengths away from the spot where it has landed – but no nearer the hole – and then, holding your ball at shoulder height, drop it on to the ground. Now take your shot but remember you will incur a one-stroke penalty and you must add this to your score.

FIND OUT MORE

Governing Organizations

The Royal and Ancient Golf Club of St Andrews
Fife, Scotland, KY16 9JD;
tel: 01334 460000,
www.randa.org
The governing body for the rules of the game.

Professional Golfers' Association (UK)
Centenary House, The De Vere Belfry, Sutton Coldfield, West Midlands, B76 9P
Tel: 01675 470333
www.pga.org.uk

Professional Golfers' Association (USA)
www.pga.com
Gives details of news, tournaments, merchandise, shows, events and PGA golf schools.

PGA European Tour
www.europeantour.com
Information, statistics and news about the European Tour.

Golf Magazines

Golf Digest
The Golf Digest Companies, 20 Westport Road, PO Box 850, Wilton, Connecticut 06897, USA; tel: 203 761 5100
www.golfdigest.com
The major American golf magazine.

Golf World, Today's Golfer, Golf Monthly, Golf Weekly, Women and Golf Magazine
Bushfield House, Orton Centre, Peterborough, PE2 5UW;
tel: 01733 237111
www.emap.com

Internet Resources

David Leadbetter Golf Academy
www.davidleadbetter.com

ESPN
Information on top players, tournaments, golf courses, etc.
www.espn.go.com

Golf Today
Online golfing magazine with
weekly bulletins and golf
news.
www.golftoday.co.uk

WorldGolf.com
An online golf publication
which lists golf schools
around the world.
www.worldgolf.com

Other golf books from HarperCollins

Andrisani, John, *Play Golf like Tiger Woods* (HarperCollins)

Dear, Tony, *Good Golf Made Easy* (HarperCollins)

Els, Ernie, with Newell, Steve, *The Complete Short Game*
(HarperCollins)

Els, Ernie, with Newell, Steve, *How to Build a Classic Swing*
(HarperCollins)

Golf World, *Improve Your Golf* (HarperCollins)

Jacobs, John, with Newell, Steve, *50 Greatest Golf Lessons of the
Century* (HarperCollins)

Lawrensen, Derek, *Sunday Telegraph Golf Course Guide*
(HarperCollins)

Leadbetter, David, *Faults and Fixes* (HarperCollins)

Leadbetter, David, *The Fundamentals of Hogan* (HarperCollins)

Leadbetter, David, *Golf Swing* (HarperCollins)

Leadbetter, David, with Simmons, Richard, *100% Golf*
(HarperCollins)

Leadbetter, David, *Positive Practice* (HarperCollins)

Newell, Steve, *A Round with the Tour Pros* (HarperCollins)

Parr, Sandy, *A Little Book of Golf* (HarperCollins)

Sanderson, Sarah, *Shape up Your Golf* (HarperCollins)

Vickers, Jonathan, *Pocket Golf Rules* (HarperCollins)

www.getmapping.com, *Golf Courses* (HarperCollins)

GLOSSARY

Above ground: A ball is above ground when it is not settled down in the rough, in a bunker or other hazard.

Alignment: The relationship between the line to the target and the golfer's body.

Approach: A shot that is played to the green.

Apron: The grass surrounding the green that is not as short as the green but is shorter than the fairway.

At rest: When the ball has stopped moving.

Backspin: Impart a backward spinning rotation to the ball to make it fly high and grip the turf when it strikes the ground to minimize bounce.

Bunker: A shallow or deep impression usually filled with sand, although it may be filled with grass or earth.

Carry: The distance to where the ball lands from which it is played.

Chip: A short, low running approach shot to the green.

Choke down: To take your grip lower on the club to get more control or less length.

Cocking the wrists: The bend or break in the wrists on the backswing.

Divot: The piece of turf that is dug out by the club.

Downhill lie: When the ball is hit from a downslope.

Fade: A shot that is hit from left to right.

Fat: When the head of an iron hits the turf before the ball, preventing it reaching target.

Ground under repair: A part of the course that is marked as being unfit for play.

Hook: A shot that causes the ball to curve to the left.

Lie: The relationship between the position of the ball and the ground underneath it.

Loose impediments: Natural objects, such as stones, leaves, branches and worms, which can be removed except in a hazard (bunker or water).

Mishit: A shot that is not hit exactly in the centre of the club face.

Obstructions: A man-made or artificial object on the course.

Out-of-bounds: A ball that falls outside the boundaries of the course, or where play is prohibited.

Par: The estimated standard score for a hole, which is usually based on its length.

Penalty stroke: A stroke or strokes that are added to a player's score when they commit a breach of the Rules.

Pitch: A high shot played from around the green, possibly over a bunker, to the hole.

Pitch and run: This is lower than a pitch shot and, on landing short of the green, runs on towards the hole.

Pitch mark: The dent or the indentation that is caused by a ball landing on the green.

Plugged ball: A ball resting in a depression in a bunker or the rough made on landing.

Pull: A shot that flies to the left of target.

Push: A shot that flies to the right of target.

Rough: Grass that has been permitted to grow to penalize shots that are hit off-line.

Scratch: A golfer with a handicap of zero.

Semi-rough: The grass growing between the uncut rough and the fairway.

Shank: When a ball is hit with an iron at the spot where the shaft joins the head, creating a shot played at right angles.

Sidespin: This may be right-to-left or left-to-right rotation of the ball to create a shot that bends to the left or right.

Sky: When the ball is struck by a wood on the top edge of the club causing it to fly upwards.

Slice: A ball that is hit in such a way that it flies in a curve to the right of target.

Stance: The way the feet are placed before playing a shot.

Sweet spot: A point, usually in the centre of the club face, which, when it hits the ball, will make it travel further than if hit elsewhere.

Topspin: Spin caused by a ball being struck above the centre.

Trajectory: The flight of the golf ball.

Waggle: The movement of the club backwards and forwards before playing a shot.

INDEX

Whatever your hobby or interest, Collins has the perfect book for you. For information about Collins books visit our website: www.collins.co.uk

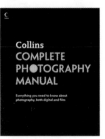

The comprehensive guide to photography in all formats.
256pp | HB | £25
ISBN 978 0 00 724394 5

Practical and inspiring advice on using colour from expert artist Shirley Trevena.
128pp | HB | £17.99
ISBN 978 0 00 722523 1

From 'can't run' to 'can't stop', this friendly guide will be your ideal training partner.
192pp | PB | £9.99
ISBN 978 0 00 723631 2

Whether you're making your first feature or just recording baby's first steps, this little book will help you avoid the pitfalls and shoot like a pro.
192pp | PB | £4.99
ISBN 978 0 00 723161 4

To order any of these titles please telephone **0870 787 1732**